Economic Development and Population Control

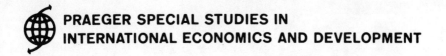

PRAEGER SPECIAL STUDIES IN
INTERNATIONAL ECONOMICS AND DEVELOPMENT

Economic Development and Population Control

A FIFTY-YEAR PROJECTION FOR JAMAICA

B. Thomas Walsh

PRAEGER PUBLISHERS
New York • Washington • London

The purpose of Praeger Special Studies is to make specialized research in U.S. and international economics and politics available to the academic, business, and government communities. For further information, write to the Special Projects Division, Praeger Publishers, Inc., 111 Fourth Avenue, New York, N.Y. 10003.

PRAEGER PUBLISHERS
111 Fourth Avenue, New York, N.Y. 10003, U.S.A.
5, Cromwell Place, London S.W.7, England

Published in the United States of America in 1971
by Praeger Publishers, Inc.

ACKNOWLEDGMENTS

The author wishes to express his appreciation for the
privilege of working closely with a number of colleagues and
specialists in the areas of demography and economic development. Principally responsible for helping guide the study
into its present form were Dr. Saul M. Katz, Director of
Economic and Social Development, Graduate School of Public
and International Affairs, and Dr. Mark Perlman, Chairman
of the Economics Department, University of Pittsburgh.
Special thanks are owed to John C. Cutler, M. D., Director
of the Population Division, Graduate School of Public Health,
for his encouragement and support.

Much helpful advice was received from Dr. Richard W.
Hooley and Dr. Huntley G. Manhertz, who critically reviewed
the manuscript. Additional insights were given me in demog-
raphy and manpower by Dr. Arthur M. Conning and Dr. Jay
Buffenmyer. I also wish to express thanks for editorial
assistance to Dr. Helen Jean Moore, Librarian at Point Park
College. Lastly, the author wishes to express his thanks to
Carolyn K. Spillane for her skilled typing and secretarial help.

CONTENTS

LIST OF TABLES

LIST OF FIGURES

Economic Development and Population Control

CHAPTER 1 INTRODUCTION

THE SIGNIFICANCE OF THE STUDY

As the 1960's moved to a close, many of the developing countries of the world embarked on a critical reexamination of their policies for economic development. Far too often, economic growth rates barely kept pace with population growth. The optimism of the "development decade" was replaced by a disillusionment in the efficacy of economic plans and policies. Failure to attain rapid economic growth was often attributed to weaknesses in the planning process itself. Greater realism, particularly in regard to the scarcity of capital, caused a scaling down of economic goals.

Many developing countries experienced turmoil and instability as their peoples demanded that governments become responsive in fulfilling aspirations for a better way of life. Problems of unemployment and underemployment served to divert scarce resources that might otherwise be used for development. The inability to meet satisfactorily the needs of ever-increasing populations served as impetus to adoption of national family planning programs in more than thirty of the developing countries.

Such actions marked a break with the belief that the modernization process is sufficient to bring about a transition to lower fertility rates. Historically, the advent of industrialization, growth of literacy, development of a middle class, and other features of modernization were considered necessary preconditions to a demographic transition--that is, a transition to a population condition in which lowered death rates are followed by reduced fertility rates. The economic frustration experienced by many countries and the perception that economic progress attained was not keeping pace with population directed concern toward policies limiting the rate of population growth. The concept of hastening modernization by reversing the cause-effect relationship with fertility decline appeared as a reasonable alternative in many developing countries.

This study seeks to extend this concept by systematically exploring--for a developing country--the implications of lower rates of population growth for several major economic growth variables. The problem is investigated through construction of a demographic-econometric model that simulates the economy of a representative country under varying fertility assumptions and under conditions reflecting changes in productivity and shifts in the structure of the economy.

The construction of a model helps to make clear the results of interactions that cannot be adequately and systematically handled by a descriptive approach alone. Most descriptive analyses utilize unicausal relationships and rarely become involved in complex systems of interdependent relationships. The use of models, on the other hand, allows the exploration of interdependent relationships. Relationships studied here are those that represent, systematically, the effects of size of population on economic development.

Because of the availability and reliability of demographic and economic data, Jamaica was chosen as a case example. The use of Jamaican data adds a dimension of realism to the model in that, as far as possible, coefficients and parameters are derived from time series analysis and all base data are actual. In consequence, although some of the quantitative conclusions cannot be applied to countries other than Jamaica without further specific investigations, the analytical methods evolved and most of the qualitative conclusions have general application.

The objective of this study is to gather and analyze support for the thesis that economic growth in a developing country can be substantially increased and accelerated by reductions in fertility rates.

BASIC FEATURES

Conclusions are based on demographic and economic projections for Jamaica covering a fifty-year period--from 1970 through 2020. Population growth is estimated under four fertility assumptions: constant, and reduced by 1, 2, and 3 percent a year. The latter is the rate needed to bring about "zero" growth in the period following the close of the century. Estimates are included of numbers of individuals needed to accept effective contraceptive methods to reduce births to stipulated levels of fertility.

The economic part of the model considers effects on production due to the amount of capital and labor available, changes
in the capital-labor ratio (factor returns), economies of scale,
and technological progress. Important features not previously
incorporated within a single model include the costs of a fertility reduction program and other welfare expenditures and
the effect of changes in the capital-labor ratio on employment.
Savings are made a function of total income and of increases
in consumption brought about by net additions to the population.
Consumption is calculated on the basis of equivalent adult consumers.

The economic relationships are described by a series of
simultaneous equations containing twenty economic variables.
Estimates, on a yearly basis, are made for gross national
product; private, public, and total consumption in aggregate
and per equivalent adult consumer; gross domestic savings;
foreign savings; gross domestic investment; demographic investment; welfare investment; net fixed total and productive
capital formation; stock of total and productive capital; capital
consumption allowance; imports minus exports; net foreign
transfer payments; and the capital-labor ratio.

There is no intent to construct a complete econometric
model of an economy. Of necessity, simplifying assumptions
have been made concerning certain economic interrelationships
that are not systematically related to the rate of growth or size
of population. Similarily, considerations of the broader social,
cultural, and political factors are left to one side since they
are not direct and measurable aspects of population growth.

The whole investigation is directed to analyzing the effects
of population growth on economic growth. For several decades,
in Jamaica as well as other developing countries, changes in
fertility and mortality due to advances in public health and
sanitation have far outweighed changes due to improvements
in economic conditions. Several noted demographer-economists
have advanced the opinion that the rate of population growth in
developing countries is largely independent of their rate of
economic growth.[1]

Throughout this study, in all matters of interpretation and
judgment, the most conservative course has been followed.
This bias works to the disadvantage of the lower fertility projections by underestimating the benefits to economic growth
accruing to reduced fertility. However, it strengthens the
conclusions reached since the degree of advantage demonstrated
is unlikely to be overstated.

Projections are in no sense to be construed as predictions

of what Jamaica's future will be. They are attempts to isolate
quantitatively, and to evaluate, the differential effects of alternative fertility rates on the economy within a plausible range of
values of the more important economic growth characteristics.

CHOICE OF DEMOGRAPHIC-ECONOMETRIC MODEL

Models seeking to quantify the effects of reduced fertility
on economic growth have generally taken one of three approaches:
(a) an investment model approach, in which population is treated
like any other economic project in terms of benefits and costs,[2]
(b) the growth model approach using the Harrod-Domar production function, in which increases in output are related only
to increases to capital by means of the capital output ratio,[3]
and (c) the neoclassical growth model approach, in which the
contribution of labor as well as capital is considered in the
production function.[4] There have also been efforts at a recon-
ciliation of these approaches, although no appropriate model
has been developed.[5] A careful review of the contributions
made indicates clearly that all approaches are measuring the
same benefits.

The major critical difference of the investment model
approach from the others is the use of a discounting procedure.
This procedure is based on estimating the value of a birth prevented now in terms of future consumption needs foregone.
The consumption and productivity streams of an unborn child
are worked out with appropriate rates of discount, and the
productivity stream is subtracted from the consumption stream
to get the net economic benefits of preventing a birth. Consumption is calculated from time of birth and is equal to the
consumption level of the individual's cohorts. The productivity
stream starts at a later period, generally fifteen years, and
represents the value added to output by an additional worker.

There is, however, a built-in bias in this approach because (a) average consumption is compared with marginal
productivity, (b) there is a time lag in discounting periods
between consumption and production, and (c) consumption is
treated only as a cost, even though some additional economic
activity results from it. There are also difficulties in determining appropriate rates of discount, and the process itself
almost automatically eliminates long-run considerations from
the analysis.

In growth models using the Harrod-Domar approach, the

assumption is made that the chief restriction on the growth of total output is the supply of capital. The neoclassical assumption of perfect substitutability of capital for labor, or vice-versa, is discarded. Rather, the starting point is the assumption of fixed technical coefficients so that aggregate output is related to the stock of capital by the capital output ratio, or "capital coefficient." Output is increased only if the capital stock is increased; the implicit assumptions are that there is always enough labor supply to staff the capital equipment and that any excess of labor over the needed amount has zero productivity. Such models are usually concerned with the problem of the rate of economic growth required to sustain full employment and with the relationships among income, investment, and savings, if this condition is to be achieved.

Implicit in the discussion of capital requirements is that the ratio of labor force to population and of consuming units to population does not change. Since, indeed, both proportions do change under varying fertility assumptions, the applicability of Harrod-Domar models when dynamic demographic changes are occurring is questionable.

The third approach is the neoclassical growth model. Because the full impact of demographic changes on economic variables cannot be assessed over a short period of time, it becomes important to take cognizance of changes in the labor supply and to provide a framework for considering laws of factor returns and economies of scale. Such a framework can be provided through use of a neoclassical growth model that utilizes the Cobb-Douglas production function. This function allows for both capital and labor to contribute positively to output. It has been widely used in both theoretical and empirical investigations for forty years, but its use in demographic-econometric studies is of recent origin.

Reasons for the increased use of the Cobb-Douglas production function have been suggested on the grounds that, when the purpose is to forecast the effect of changes in demographic variables over an extended period of time, the neoclassical growth model, incorporating the assumption of continuous well-behaved production functions, may be appropriate. By recognizing that the marginal productivity of labor need not be zero, the savings function need not be regarded as the only mechanism that affects economic growth.

Use of the Cobb-Douglas production function permits consideration of five economic variables: (a) labor, (b) capital, (c) factor returns, (d) economies of scale or output, and (e) innovations (broadly interpreted). By contrast, the Harrod-Domar function does not consider (a) and (c) and covers only partially (d) and (e).

The heart of any economic growth model is the mechanism
employed to determine levels of output (or income). The importance of being able to incorporate these five variables in
the Jamaica model is worth review.

Taking the first two variables together, capital and labor,
one can say that the total real income of a country will be a
function of the stock and quality of wealth and the size and efficiency of the labor force. Wealth, however, covers stocks
of all concrete things directly or indirectly used to produce
utility and includes natural resources as well as capital. Land
and other natural resources are already in existence, and, except to the extent they are exhausted, the variable part of wealth
is regarded as capital, even when it consists of man-made improvements to land. New land brought into use will require
labor and some capital in the form of machines and other
materials.

Capital rather than wealth is used as a determinant of output (or income). For one thing, the stock of natural resources
is considered to be fixed, and additions to wealth are denoted
by increases in net investment (capital). Further, to make an
estimate for all wealth is virtually impossible, since this includes land not yet explored or assessed and natural resources
not yet discovered. Capital, in consequence, becomes the
significant variable in economic analysis.

The third economic variable incorporated in the neoclassical growth model is that of factor returns. The law of factor
returns is concerned with changes in the ratio of output to the
input of a factor (capital or labor) as its quantity is increased
in relation to another factor and with whether the ratio remains
constant, increases, or decreases. Concern is with quantity
relationships. No change is assumed in the qualities of the
factors used. (Allowance for qualitative improvement resulting
from advances in technology are discussed in the section dealing with innovations.) Experience, in general, for developing
countries has been that for both labor and capital as a whole,
diminishing factor returns are likely to apply.

The fourth variable considered is the extent of economies
of scale because of increased output. Here, both labor and
capital can be considered together in answering the question
whether an increase in total output will increase production
per head. The result will be affected not only by the law of
factor returns but by changes in the proportions of the factors
as their quantities increase. An increase in total output may
permit a better combination of factors and promote other economies as well. The main concern of this study is whether output

per capita increases or decreases as a result of population
growth. Thus results must be compared according to whether
or not increases in population are accompanied by corresponding increases in capital.

If the rate of capital growth exceeds the rate of population
growth, the situation is made favorable to economies of scale.
An increase in the capital-labor ratio implies a greater availability of capital than heretofore. Capital may thus be used
to finance types of enterprise conducive to economies of scale
and which utilize a higher level of technology than those presently existing. A higher capital-labor ratio generally implies
a decline in the relative importance of agriculture and an increase in the relative importance of manufacturing, including
the use of social overhead. Thus, the direct benefits of having
more capital to work with have a cumulative influence through
the structural changes they induce (accompanied by a fuller
utilization of labor) and the capacity to create additional investment from the increased income.

It is quite unlikely that economies of scale from population
increases alone will occur in underdeveloped countries. (Those
that have abundant unused natural resources and are sparsely
settled are less dependent on creation of man-made capital
and could, in the short-run, have increasing returns to scale
for population.) In general, though, it is unlikely that levels
of consumption will rise, exclusive of innovations, if the rate
of capital growth is less than the rate of population growth.
As this study seeks to demonstrate, the benefits resulting from
more capital are normally greater if the rate of population
growth is slower.

The last type of economic variable considered in neoclassical growth models is innovations. The effect of innovations
is to increase the output obtainable with a unit of labor, capital,
or land. To isolate this factor is sometimes difficult because
technological progress can be embodied both in capital and
labor. When explicitly expressed in a production function,
rather than subsumed under other factors, innovation is generally expressed as a function of time. This study assumes
an annual compounded increase in productivity of 1.5 percent.[6]
Innovations are assumed to be neutral, equally saving of both
labor and capital.

NOTES

1. Simon Kuznets, "Demographic Aspects of Modern
Economic Growth" (working paper of the World Population
Conference in Belgrade, 1965, WPC/WP/389), p. 20; Paul
Demeny, "Investment Allocation and Population Growth, "
Demography, II (1965), 210-11; George Zaidan and E. K.
Hawkins, "The Treatment of Population in Bank Economic
Work, " Economics Department Working Paper No. 16 (Wash-
ington, D.C.: International Bank for Reconstruction and De-
velopment, 1968), p. 3; Gunnar Myrdal, Asian Drama (3 vols.;
New York: Pantheon Books Division of Random House, 1968),
II, p. 1463.

2. Stephen Enke, "The Economic Aspects of Slowing Population Growth, " The Economic Journal, LXXVI (March, 1966),
44-56; Stephen Enke, Economics for Development (Englewood
Cliffs, N.J.: Prentice-Hall, 1963), pp. 368-84; Stephen Enke,
Lower Birth Rates--Some Economic Aspects (Washington,
D.C.: United States Agency for International Development,
1965); Goran Ohlin, Population Control and Economic Development (Paris: Development Center of the Organization for Economic Cooperation and Development, 1967), pp. 107-20; Richard
L. Meier, Modern Science and the Human Fertility Problem
(New York: John Wiley and Sons, Inc., 1959); George Zaidan,
"The Foregone Benefits and Costs of a Prevented Birth: Conceptual Problems and an Application to the U.A.R., " Economics
Department Working Paper No. 11 (Washington, D.C.: International Bank for Reconstruction and Development, 1968); Zaidan
and Hawkins, op. cit.; Gerald L. Fox, "The Net Costs to Society
of a Marginal Birth in Underdeveloped Countries" (paper presented at Annual Meeting of the Population Association of America, Atlantic City, N.J., April 12, 1969).

3. Ansley J. Coale and Edgar M. Hoover, Population
Growth and Economic Development in Low Income Countries
(Princeton, N.J.: Princeton University Press, 1958); Edgar
M. Hoover and Mark Perlman, "Measuring the Effects of
Population Control on Economic Development: Pakistan as a
Case Study, " Pakistan Development Review, VI, 4 (Winter,
1966), 545-66; Demeny, op. cit., 203-32. Criticism of some
growth model studies using the Harrod-Domar production
function, notably that of Coale and Hoover, has been made by
the following: Myrdal, op. cit., III, pp. 2068-75; Simon Kuznets,
"Population and Economic Growth, " Proceedings of the American Philosophical Society, III, 3 (June, 1967), 170-93; Demeny,

op. cit.; David E. Horlacher, "Measuring the Economic Bene-
fits of Population Control: A Critical Review of the Literature, "
Penn State--USAID Working Paper No. 2 (Washington, D.C.:
United States Agency for International Development, 1968).

    4. Peter Newman and R. H. Allen, Population Growth
Rates and Economic Development in Nicaragua (Washington,
D.C.: Robert R. Nathan Associates, Inc., 1967); Stephen
Enke and Richard G. Zind, "Effect of Fewer Births on Average
Income, " Journal of Biosocial Sciences, I, 1 (1969), 41-55.
Originally published by Enke as Raising Per Capita Income
Through Fewer Births (Santa Barbara, Calif.: TEMPO, Gen-
eral Electric Center for Advanced Studies, 1967); Stephen
Enke, gen. ed., and William E. McFarland, et al., Description
of the Economic Demographic Model (Santa Barbara, Calif.:
TEMPO, General Electric Center for Advanced Studies, 1969);
Theodore K. Ruprecht, "Fertility Control, Investment and
Per Capita Output: A Demographic Econometric Model of the
Philippines, " Contributed Papers, International Union for the
Scientific Study of Population, Sydney Conference, August 21-
25, 1967, pp. 98-107; Peter Lloyd, "A Growth Model with
Population and Technological Change as Endogenous Variables."
Unpublished paper, 1968, excerpted by Warren C. Robinson
and David E. Horlacher in "Evaluating the Economic Benefits
of Fertility Reduction, " Studies in Family Planning, 39 (March,
1969), pp. 4-8.

    5. J. L. Simon "The Value of Avoided Births to Under-
developed Countries." Unpublished paper, 1967, summarized
by David E. Horlacher in "Measuring the Economic Benefits
of Population Control: A Critical Review of the Literature, "
Penn State--USAID Working Paper No. 2 (Washington, D.C.:
United States Agency for International Development, 1968),
pp. 43-45; Leonard G. Bower, "The Return from Investment
in Population Control in Less-Developed Countries, " Demography,
V, 1 (1968), 422-32; Warren C. Robinson, "Conceptual and
Methodological Problems Connected with Cost-Effectiveness
Studies of Family Planning Programs, " Penn State--USAID
Working Paper No. 1 (Washington, D.C.: United States Agency
for International Development, 1968); Paul Demeny, "The
Economics of Population Control" (paper presented at Annual
Meeting of the International Union for the Scientific Study of
Population, London, September 3-10, 1969).

    6. Enke and Zind, op. cit.

2

THE MODEL:
DEMOGRAPHIC
RELATIONSHIPS

Estimates of future population growth are basic to economic and social planning. Population projections indicate needs in such areas as education, health, housing, and employment and can be utilized in the formation of a country's population policy.

Heretofore, population growth has generally been considered an exogenous factor in development planning. The rapid improvements and more ready availability of family planning methods, however, now permit assumptions on planned changes in fertility rates that could not have been contemplated even ten years ago.

DEMOGRAPHIC TRANSITION AND ITS APPLICATION TO JAMAICA

Theorists of demographic transition have postulated that the decline in mortality in an area or country brought about by industrialization and modernization will bring about a decline in fertility. Whether this theory, based on the experience of the developed countries in the last century, is applicable to underdeveloped countries today is very uncertain. There is nothing in the theory of demographic transition that states precisely what conditions are essential for a fertility decline nor whether these conditions will be present in a developing area at a certain time. Perhaps, the decline in mortality may in itself provide a sufficient cause for fertility reduction. The desire to ensure family continuity and obtain support for old age can be satisfied with a smaller number of births, especially since much of the mortality decline typically occurs in childhood.

Experience on this score is discouraging, however. In most underdeveloped countries that have had substantial

declines in the death rate, fertility declines, if any, have
lagged by at least one generation. A reduction in mortality
rates, especially for infants and children, results in larger
numbers of females reaching, and passing through, the childbearing ages. This means that even if age-specific birth rates
remain at the same levels, the number of births increases because there are more women of childbearing ages.

Though the time since World War II is a somewhat short
period from which to deduce future trends in developing countries, evidence indicates that fertility, in the absence of effective programs for family planning, remains at traditionally
high levels or may even increase slightly, whether or not
there is economic development.

Jamaica is interesting to study because, though population
trends have changed markedly, demographic transition has
failed to move past the first stage: mortality has declined;
fertility has not declined. From 1844, the year of the first
census, through World War I, Jamaica was characterized by
high fertility and high mortality. Commencing in the 1920's,
however, mortality steadily declined. Before 1921, crude
death rates never fell below twenty-three per 1000; the average
during 1921-43 was eighteen, with the trend continuing downward. The crude birth rate also declined from thirty-seven
to thirty-three in this same period.

The seeming transition to lower fertility rates was short-
lived. After World War II, birth rates climbed back to those
prevailing in 1921. The average between 1953 and 1960 was
thirty-seven per 1000. Since 1960, the crude birth rate has
averaged over forty. Postwar death rates have averaged
twelve, as compared with eighteen in the 1921-43 period. The
resulting rate of natural increase for 1943-60, therefore,
was 2.3 percent per year, which was markedly higher than
ever before. In the 1960's, the rate of natural increase surged
to 3.2 percent.

MIGRATION IN JAMAICA

A third variable affecting size and structure of a given
population in addition to fertility and mortality is migration.
Despite the relative past importance of migration on population
growth in Jamaica, this factor is not included in the model.
Several reasons can be advanced for this decision. First, all
other demographic-econometric studies have operated under

the same decision; therefore, comparability with these studies can be enhanced by exclusion of this factor. Second, only the most speculative type of projection would be possible because control over future migration policies is in the hands of recipient countries. Third, the level of migration cannot be quantitatively related to differences in fertility. Higher population growth rates may create "push" factors encouraging migration, but the willingness of other countries and the economic opportunities found there, i.e., "pull" factors, are the more likely determinants of migration.

One would speculate that future trends in migration will be downward. Worldwide, immigration policies have tended to become more restrictive as internal population problems become more readily apparent. The encouragement of migration to relieve population pressures is only a palliative; long-term solutions involve bringing internal growth rates under control.

The likelihood that the future effects of migration will be diminishing permits it to be omitted from the model without altering substantially the validity of the projections. Further, since only one range of slightly declining mortality is postulated for the model, the differences observed in the projections primarily reflect changes in fertility. The inclusion of population changes from migration for analytical purposes may, therefore, tend to obscure, somewhat, the effects due to fertility changes.

DEMOGRAPHIC INPUTS OF THE MODEL

The factor of migration being excluded, the demographic inputs of the model are based on fertility and mortality. Overall, the model provides projections of Jamaican population by age and sex at five-year intervals through 2020. Base population is derived from census data of 1960, with ages grouped by five-year cohorts. The number, age, and sex of persons surviving through each succeeding five-year interval are estimated by use of age- and sex-specific survival rates. Likewise, births in each five-year interval are estimated through the use of age-specific birth rates for women in the childbearing ages (fifteen to forty-nine).

Birth and survival rates used are adjusted from interval to interval, according to a pattern that corresponds to a set of stipulated demographic assumptions. No abrupt changes in fertility or mortality are postulated.

Base Population

The first data requirement for the demographic part of
the model is the initial population of the country, giving age
composition by five-year cohorts and sex composition. Although census and vital statistics data for Jamaica are more
complete and reliable than for most developing countries, a
number of adjustments were needed in order to enter demographic data into the model. A brief description of the procedures followed indicates some of the basic problems of data
handling that will be encountered in any demographic-econometric study using actual data.

At the time Jamaica data utilized here were being col-
lected, 1966 marked the last full year for which demographic
and economic data were available. Some preliminary estimates
for 1967 had been made, but these were subject to later revisions. In consequence, the first outputs generated by the
model were for 1967.

General practice is to estimate demographic outputs by
five-year intervals. In order to maintain a balance between
needed simplicity and desired approximation to actual facts,
fertility and mortality rates are assumed constant within each
successive five-year interval. Mid-year estimates of population by age and sex are produced for the year marking the end
of each five-year interval (i. e., 1970, 1975, 1980, and so
forth).

Because economic outputs are generated on a single year
basis, demographic outputs on the same basis had to be provided. Changes by age and sex for each five-year interval
were prorated for each single year. Since slightly more births
and deaths occur in the latter half of any given interval, an
adjustment using Lagrange integers was employed to reflect
this difference.

The first projection year of the model, 1967, is within
the five-year interval 1965-70. The use of the estimated
mean population of 1965 by age and sex as the base demographic
data is, therefore, indicated. To do so, it was necessary to
go back to the last enumeration reflecting age-sex composition
in Jamaica, the census of April 7, 1960.

After completion of the 1960 census, the Department of
Statistics carefully analyzed the results and made appropriate
revisions. Adjustment was made for underenumeration in the
0-4 age group for males and females, as reflected by cross-
check with the Registrar General's Office. (The increase
arises from differences at ages zero and one only.) The

enumerated population showed a tendency, more pronounced among females than males, favoring age intervals ending five to nine at the expense of the zero to four age interval that follows. By use of a balancing equation, smoothing was done for male groups forty to sixty-nine and female groups from thirty-five to sixty-nine. Because the factor of emigration was considered sufficiently important, no smoothing was attempted for the younger ages, where migration was most prevalent. Nor was smoothing attempted for the population aged seventy years and older, because reporting is considered quite inaccurate for these ages.

Revised census figures give Jamaica a population of 1,624,400 for 1960. Such figures do not properly reflect the estimated mid-year population for that year since the census was taken as of April 7. Mean population was calculated, therefore, by adding births between April 7 and June 30 and subtracting deaths and net migration for the same period. The estimated population, as of June 30, 1960, is set at 1,628,200.

The ratio of the estimated mid-year population to the revised census estimate of April 7 was $\frac{1,628,200}{1,624,400} = 1.00234$. Mid-year estimates by age and sex were obtained by multiplying the respective census data by this ratio, with the results indicated in Table 1.

Births, deaths, and net migration are recorded on a calendar year basis, reported as year-end totals, in Table 2. Population estimates are likewise reported as of the end of the year.

Survival Rates

The second demographic input needed for the model is survival rates. The rates represent the proportion of a population in a particular five-year age cohort that survives from the beginning to the end of a five-year interval. The exception is the infant survival rate, which is the proportion of live births during a five-year interval surviving to the end of the interval.

In this study, the first step was to determine for Jamaica appropriate survival rates for the base period, 1965-70. The second step was to ascertain what pattern of mortality would most likely take place in subsequent years. Only one best assumption of future mortality experience is postulated for the model.

TABLE 1

Estimated Mean Population, by Sex and Age, Jamaica, 1960

Age Groups	Census of April 7, 1960 (Revised)[a]			Estimated Mean Population (June 30, 1960)[b]		
	Males	Females	Total	Males	Females	Total
All Ages	781,190	843,210	1,624,400	783,020	845,180	1,628,200
0-4	142,700	139,780	282,480	143,030	140,110	283,140
5-9	110,920	109,770	220,690	111,180	110,030	221,210
10-14	86,740	87,180	173,920	86,950	87,380	174,330
15-19	68,370	76,440	144,810	68,530	76,620	145,150
20-24	56,830	68,040	124,870	59,960	68,200	125,160
25-29	49,680	61,390	111,070	49,800	61,530	111,330
30-34	42,830	51,070	93,900	42,930	51,190	94,120
35-39	41,230	49,050	90,280	41,330	49,160	90,490
40-44	39,630	41,720	81,350	39,720	41,820	81,540
45-49	38,900	39,070	77,970	38,990	39,160	78,150
50-54	32,900	33,620	66,520	32,980	33,700	66,680
55-59	23,570	24,510	48,080	23,630	24,560	48,190
60-64	18,360	20,430	38,790	18,400	20,480	38,880
65-69	10,110	12,500	22,610	10,130	12,530	22,660
70-74	8,100	11,210	19,310	8,120	11,240	19,360
75-79	5,110	7,720	12,830	5,120	7,740	12,860
80+	5,210	9,710	14,920	5,220	9,730	14,950

[a]From first source cited below.
[b]From second source cited below.

Sources: Adapted from University of the West Indies, Estimates of Intercensal Population by Age and Sex and Revised Vital Rates for British Caribbean Countries, 1946-1960, Census Research Program Publication No. 8 (Kingston, 1964); Jamaica Registrar General, Demographic Statistics of Jamaica, 1964 (Spanishtown, 1965).

17

TABLE 2

Vital Statistics, Jamaica, 1959-67

Births, Deaths, and Net Migration	1959	1960	1961	1962	1963	1964	1965	1966	1967
Live Births	63,824	68,413	66,128	64,913	66,189	68,359	69,768	71,364	67,438
Deaths:	16,550	14,321	14,193	14,167	15,159	13,267	14,084	14,288	13,295
Natural Increase	47,274	54,092	51,935	50,746	51,030	55,092	55,684	57,076	54,143
Net Migration:	13,070	30,346	38,540	28,701	7,279	13,491	7,047	8,867	20,138
Population Increase	34,204	23,746	13,395	22,045	43,751	41,601	48,637	48,209	34,005
Estimated Population:									
At End of Year	1,615,100	1,638,900	1,652,300	1,674,300	1,718,100	1,759,700	1,810,900	1,859,100	1,893,100
Mean Population	1,598,400	1,628,200	1,646,200	1,659,800	1,696,500	1,739,800	1,788,200	1,836,700	1,876,400
Per 1,000 Mean Population:									
Birth Rate	39.93	42.02	40.17	39.11	39.02	39.24	39.02	38.85	35.94
Death Rate	10.35	8.79	8.62	8.54	8.94	7.74	7.88	7.78	7.09
Infant Deaths (Under 1 year of age)	4,458	3,522	3,227	3,168	3,379	2,599	2,612	2,524	2,057
Infant Death Rate (Per 1,000 live births)	69.86	51.48	48.80	47.31	49.28	39.31	37.44	35.37	30.50

Sources: Jamaica Department of Statistics, Annual Abstract of Statistics, 1967, No. 26 (Kingston, December, 1967), Table 19; Jamaica Registrar General, Demographic Statistics of Jamaica, 1967 (Spanishtown, May, 1968); Jamaica Department of Statistics, Quarterly Abstract of Statistics, Nos. 8, 13, 21, and 26 (Kingston, December, 1962; March, 1964; March, 1966; and June, 1967).

Choice of model life tables was between those of the United
Nations (U.N.) and sets of regional life tables developed by
Coale and Demeny.[1] The Coale-Demeny life tables differ from
those of the U.N. in that they comprise four regional sets
rather than one worldwide set. The use of region "West"
model life tables is particularly suggested for underdeveloped
countries. The Coale-Demeny life tables comprise twenty-
four levels of mortality experience, with a maximum combined
expectation of life at birth ($^{0}e_{0}$) of 75.7 years. Initial survival
rates for the 1965-70 period were interpolated between levels
twenty and twenty-one of the Coale-Demeny, Model "West"
tables. Allowance was made for deviations in infant and child
mortality rates since the age reporting in these groups is considered inaccurate. For other age groups, the interpolated
Coale-Demeny values were used without further adjustment.

Mortality experience was extended on this basis for a
reasonable maximum. With the current overall expectation
of life at birth in excess of sixty-six years, future improvement in mortality experience will be, most certainly, less
than in the past. The expectation of life at birth will average
74.5 years by 1995, with no further decline postulated after
that date. Such an expectation will be at a level approximately
equal to the most favorable expectations of life for the United
States at that time. All estimated survival rates are given in
Table 3.

Age-Specific Birth Rates

The next needed demographic input for the model is levels
of fertility. Four assumptions as to the future course of
Jamaican fertility are made: the "high," "medium," "low,"
and "very low" fertility assumptions. The "high" one assumes
that age-specific birth rates will remain constant through 2020.
The "medium" one assumes that age-specific birth rates will
decline from 1970 to 2020 to one-half of initial (1965-70) age-
specific birth rates (5 percent decline per five-year period).
The "low" one assumes that age-specific birth rates will decline from 1970 to 1995 to one-half initial (1965-70) age-
specific birth rates; thereafter, it will be constant through
2020 (10 percent decline per five-year period). The "very
low" one assumes that age-specific birth rates will decline
from 1970 to 1995 so as to reach zero-growth rate in the
period 1995-2020 (15 percent decline per five-year period).

The first fertility assumption, that age-specific birth

TABLE 3

Estimation of Survival Rates in Accordance with Postulated
Assumption of Mortality Decline, by Fixed Age Groups,
Jamaica, 1965-2020

(a)

Males

Age in Years	1965-70	1970-75	1975-80	1980-85	1985-90	1990-95	1995-2020
Infants	.93925	.94763	.95486	.96109	.96452	.96912	.97307
0-4	.98359	.98635	.98863	.99051	.99206	.99334	.99440
5-9	.99644	.99719	.99778	.99824	.99860	.99887	.99910
10-14	.99628	.99702	.99762	.99811	.99850	.99882	.99908
15-19	.99397	.99522	.99621	.99699	.99761	.99810	.99849
20-24	.99168	.99346	.99485	.99594	.99679	.99745	.99797
25-29	.98977	.99188	.99356	.99490	.99596	.99681	.99748
30-34	.98678	.98930	.99135	.99302	.99438	.99548	.99637
35-39	.98074	.98392	.98658	.98880	.99066	.99221	.99351
40-44	.97165	.97560	.97900	.98193	.98445	.98661	.98847
45-49	.95544	.96020	.96445	.96824	.97162	.97464	.97733
50-54	.93191	.93767	.94295	.94779	.95222	.95627	.95998
55-59	.90043	.90746	.91400	.92008	.92573	.93098	.93585
60-64	.85112	.85905	.86654	.87361	.88028	.88657	.89249
65-69	.78527	.79485	.80403	.81282	.82123	.82928	.83697
70-74	.69020	.70241	.71417	.72549	.73637	.74682	.75685
75-79	.55545	.56683	.57787	.58857	.59893	.60895	.61864
80+	.36261	.36843	.37412	.37968	.38511	.39041	.39558

(b)

Females

Age in Years	1965-70	1970-75	1975-80	1980-85	1985-90	1990-95	1995-2020
Infants	.94920	.95682	.96329	.96857	.97322	.97715	.98048
0-4	.98639	.98887	.99090	.99256	.99392	.99503	.99594
5-9	.99704	.99774	.99827	.99867	.99897	.99920	.99937
10-14	.99633	.99716	.99780	.99829	.99867	.99896	.99918
15-19	.99391	.99526	.99631	.99713	.99777	.99826	.99864
20-24	.99229	.99401	.99535	.99639	.99720	.99783	.99832
25-29	.99063	.99258	.99411	.99531	.99625	.99699	.99757
30-34	.98777	.99000	.99182	.99330	.99451	.99550	.99631
35-39	.98291	.98552	.98777	.98971	.99138	.99282	.99406
40-44	.97683	.97993	.98262	.98495	.98697	.98872	.99024
45-49	.96711	.97082	.97410	.97700	.97956	.98182	.98382
50-54	.95165	.95602	.96000	.96362	.96692	.96992	.97265
55-59	.93167	.93705	.94200	.94655	.95073	.95457	.95810
60-64	.89990	.90696	.91353	.91964	.92532	.93059	.93549
65-69	.84960	.85927	.86832	.87678	.88469	.89207	.89896
70-74	.77181	.78444	.79641	.80774	.81846	.82859	.83815
75-79	.62192	.63113	.63992	.64830	.65629	.66389	.67112
80+	.38453	.38737	.39020	.39302	.39583	.39863	.40142

(c)

Expectation of Life at Birth

Sex Category	1965-70	1970-75	1975-80	1980-85	1985-90	1990-95	1995-2020
Male	64.18	66.02	67.67	69.15	70.35	71.55	72.63
Female	68.07	69.89	71.51	72.93	74.21	75.34	76.36
Combined	66.12	67.96	69.59	71.04	72.28	73.45	74.50

20

rates will remain high and constant throughout the projection period, is the base to which all other fertility assumptions are compared. This is a standard assumption of demographic-econometric studies and is plausible in that most developing countries have not exhibited any decline in birth rates in the period since World War II. The projection at the high, constant rate is also needed to provide a basis for calculating the expenditures needed, whether through an organized family planning program or not, to reach any stipulated level of reduction of fertility.

The medium fertility assumption of a decline of 1 percent per year for the entire projection period corresponds to the medium assumption utilized in the U.N. projections.[2] The low fertility assumption stipulates twice the rate of decline as the medium fertility alternative--2 percent a year. This rate of decline is maintained for twenty-five years only (through 1995), after which time age-specific fertility rates will remain at a level equal to one-half of the 1970 rates. This low fertility assumption also corresponds to the low assumption of U.N. studies.

A very low fertility assumption, not included in any previous demographic-econometric study, is made here to see what the effects would be if a zero-growth rate were obtained. As has been suggested by Kingsley Davis and others, serious consideration should be given by all countries of the world to the implementation of such population control programs as to reach a zero-growth rate by the end of this century.[3] How great a decline in fertility rates would be needed to achieve this condition depends on the initial fertility rates in a country, its mortality rates and likely future course, and the age-sex composition of the population.

For Jamaica, a first approximation suggests that the fertility decline needed to reach zero-growth rate after twenty-five years (1995) would be between 15 and 20 percent for each five-year period. The exact amount was solved iteratively by a subroutine in the computer and approximated 15.5 percent. Because of the short time interval in trying to reach a zero growth rate, population growth, for a time, is negative and then becomes positive. This "cycle" effect is more pronounced in the calculations: the steeper the decline to a zero-growth rate and the shorter the period after 1995 in which births and deaths are brought into balance. Since rapid fertility declines do not accord enough time for a population to stabilize into a mature pattern of age-distribution, the population, as a whole, has a low median age, and the number of deaths is considerably less than in a mature population. If fertility rates decline to a point where births approximately equal these rather low numbers of deaths, it becomes apparent shortly after that deaths increasingly overshoot the number of births. Since we are neither interested in postulating a negative population growth rate nor in advocating a reverse policy of increasing birth rates after a marked decline in fertility, it becomes apparent that a zero-growth rate should be approached gradually and averaged out over a longer period, say, twenty-five years.

Such a time span has been utilized in this model, and, although the fertility decline occurs only through 1995, the rate of decline permits a zero-growth rate to be gradually met by 2020. This time interval eliminates most of the distortion of the age-sex distribution induced by the rapid transition in fertility rates. Any swings in the population growth rate are negligible, and the stipulated levels of age-specific fertility rates will keep the size of population relatively constant after 2020.

The base inputs needed for all fertility assumptions are the 1965 age-specific birth rates. To calculate age-specific birth rates for 1965, age-specific birth rates for 1960 had to be determined. Statistics on live births by age of mother are available for 1960, but the data include a small number of mothers in the fifty to fifty-four age group and a certain number of "age unknowns." In Table 4, the births ascribed to mothers over fifty were combined into the forty-five to forty-nine age group and the "age unknown" births prorated to the other age groups.

Next, the 1960 age-specific birth rates were applied to the estimated number of women in each of the childbearing age intervals for the years 1961-65. The resultant number of births were estimated and compared to the number of births registered in each of these years. The use of 1960 rates produced an underestimate of births in each year. This difference amounted to 4.19 percent in 1965, and, thus, the 1960 rates were increased by this percent to obtain the revised 1965 age-specific birth rates, as is indicated in Table 5.

Age-specific birth rates, under varying fertility assumptions through 2020 for Jamaica, are given in Table 6. The fraction of live births that are male has been steady in Jamaica at .50496 for three decades.

TABLE 4

Age-Specific Birth Rates, Jamaica, 1960

Age Groups	Births by Age of Mother (Unadjusted)	Adjusted Births	Estimated Female Population, June 30, 1960	Age-Specific Birth Rate
10-14	86	86	87,384	1.0
15-19	11,785	11,799	76,619	154.0
20-24	20,345	20,369	68,199	298.7
25-29	16,354	16,374	61,534	266.1
30-34	10,876	10,889	51,190	212.7
35-39	6,481	6,489	49,165	132.0
40-44	2,083	2,086	41,818	49.9
45-49	290	321	39,161	8.2
50-54	31			
Unknown	82			
Total	68,413	68,413	475,070	1122.6

Source: Jamaica Department of Statistics (O. C. Francis), The People of Jamaica (Kingston, 1963), Table 5.12, "Number of Children by Age of Mother, 1960."

Outline of Demographic Inputs

To sum up, there are five types of demographic input required for programming in the model:
1. Base population--five-year age groups from zero to eighty and one group of eighty and over for both males and females
2. Survival rates--five-year age groups from zero to eighty and one group of eighty and over for both males and females for each five-year interval
3. Age-specific birth rates--five-year age groups for women fifteen to forty-nine for each five-year interval
4. Survival rates at birth--male and female
5. Fraction of live births that are male--assumed to be constant at .50496 for all intervals.

TABLE 5

Projection of Births 1961-65, Assuming
Age-Specific Birth Rates of 1960, Jamaica

Age Groups	1960 Age-Specific Birth Rates	Births					Revised Age-Specific Birth Rates, 1965
		1961	1962	1963	1964	1965	
10-14	1.0	93	97	101	106	111	
15-19	154.0	12,027	12,212	12,536	12,936	13,429	161.5
20-24	298.7	19,505	19,296	19,834	20,491	20,969	311.2
25-29	266.1	15,274	14,662	14,609	14,529	14,529	277.2
30-34	212.7	10,210	9,933	10,039	10,210	10,210	221.6
35-39	132.0	6,085	5,808	5,650	5,478	5,372	137.5
40-44	49.9	2,016	2,001	2,021	2,056	2,046	52.0
45-49	8.2	312	305	300	296	294	8.5
Total Computed Number of Births (All Ages)		65,522	64,314	65,090	66,102	66,960	
Registered Number of Births		66,128	64,913	66,189	68,359	69,768	
Percent Higher		0.92	0.93	1.69	3.41	4.19	

Source: Jamaica Department of Statistics, Annual Abstract of Statistics 1967, No. 26 (Kingston, December, 1967), Table 19.

TABLE 6

Age-Specific Birth Rates, Under Varying Fertility Assumptions, Jamaica, 1965-2020[a]

Age Groups	High Fertility 1965-2020	Medium Fertility 1965-70	1970-75	1975-80	1980-85	1985-90	1990-95	1995-2000	2000-5	2005-10	2010-15	2015-20
15-19	.1615	.1615	.1575	.1494	.1314	.1332	.1252	.1172	.1090	.1009	.0929	.0848
20-24	.3112	.3112	.3034	.2879	.2723	.2567	.2412	.2256	.2101	.1945	.1789	.1634
25-29	.2772	.2772	.2703	.2564	.2425	.2287	.2148	.2010	.1871	.1732	.1594	.1455
30-34	.2216	.2216	.2161	.2050	.1939	.1828	.1717	.1607	.1496	.1385	.1274	.1163
35-39	.1375	.1375	.1341	.1272	.1203	.1134	.1066	.0997	.0928	.0859	.0791	.0722
40-44	.0520	.0520	.0507	.0481	.0455	.0429	.0403	.0377	.0351	.0325	.0299	.0273
45-49	.0085	.0085	.0083	.0079	.0074	.0070	.0066	.0062	.0057	.0053	.0049	.0045

Low Fertility

Age Groups	1965-70	1970-75	1975-80	1980-85	1985-90	1990-95	1995-2020
15-19	.1615	.1534	.1373	.1211	.1050	.0880	.0807
20-24	.3112	.2956	.2645	.2334	.2023	.1712	.1556
25-29	.2772	.2633	.2356	.2079	.1802	.1525	.1386
30-34	.2216	.2105	.1844	.1662	.1440	.1229	.1108
35-39	.1375	.1306	.1169	.1031	.0894	.0756	.0687
40-44	.0520	.0494	.0442	.0390	.0338	.0286	.0260
45-49	.0085	.0081	.0072	.0064	.0055	.0047	.0042

Very Low Fertility

Age Groups	1965-70	1970-75	1975-80	1980-85	1985-90	1990-95	1995-2020
15-19	.1615	.1494	.1252	.1009	.0767	.0525	.0283
20-24	.3112	.2879	.2412	.1945	.1478	.1011	.0545
25-29	.2772	.2564	.2148	.1733	.1317	.0901	.0485
30-34	.2216	.2050	.1717	.1385	.1053	.0720	.0388
35-39	.1375	.1272	.1066	.0859	.0653	.0447	.0241
40-44	.0520	.0481	.0403	.0325	.0247	.0169	.0091
45-49	.0085	.0079	.0066	.0053	.0040	.0028	.0015

[a]Expressed as births per woman.

DEMOGRAPHIC OUTPUTS OF THE MODEL

In obtaining certain demographic outputs for the projection period, some of the data necessitates special handling. Estimates of population by age and sex are straightforward and need no adjustment. Additional steps, however, are needed in arriving at estimates of equivalent adult consumers, labor force, births prevented, and numbers of contraceptive acceptors needed. The kinds of adjustments made are described in the sections that follow.

Equivalent Adult Consumers

Central to the economic analysis in this study is the need to provide calculations for increases in total consumption when population increases. The proportion of population that consists of infants and children makes an obvious difference in consumption needs. Since the needs of children are substantially lower than the needs of adults, a distinction should be made between different types of increments to the population as they influence requirements for different types of goods and services.

The decision was made, therefore, to use the concept of the "equivalent adult consumer," a concept used frequently in analyses of consumers' expenditures as well as other economic studies. The basic question in determining what comprises an "equivalent adult" is the matter of determining weights. Some studies do not allow for graduations in the needs of children as they grow older; others seem to be unduly elaborate, with no substantiation that the weightings do, in fact, approximate reality.

The weightings used in this Jamaica model are closely patterned after those in the Newman-Allen study of Nicaragua. [4] Slightly higher weights for the lower age groups are used in the Jamaica model to reflect higher levels of expenditures for health and education. In Nicaragua, less than 10 percent of total public expenditure is for these purposes, but in Jamaica, such outlays consistently exceed 40 percent of total public expenditures. Since expenditures for education in particular, and for health to a lesser extent, are proportionately greater for children than for adults, it was deemed appropriate to increase the equivalent consumption weights in the younger age categories. The weights used in this study are indicated in Table 7.

TABLE 7

Weights Assigned, by Age Groups,
To Determine Equivalent Adult Consumers

Age Groups	Weights
0-4	.35
5-9	.50
10-14	.75
15+	1.00

Experimental runs were made using other sets of weight-ings. The effect on consumption from year to year was minor in all cases, and since the weights selected seemed adequate to reality, they were employed without further modification.

Calculation of the number of equivalent adult consumers and of the increase from previous years of equivalent adult consumers was necessary base year input for the model. Values obtained for 1960 through 1965 are indicated in Table 8.

Labor Force

A second demographic output requiring some adjustment arises from the definitions used for "labor force." Population projections allow for the changing age composition of a popula-tion, and, thus, for the changing number of persons of working age. Since the Jamaica model includes the contribution of labor to product, it is necessary to provide an estimate of the labor force.

The concept of a labor force originated in industrialized countries, where the distinction between employment and un-employment is much more clear-cut than in countries domi-nated by peasant agriculture. This concept normally requires the projection of the participation rate in the labor force so that a projection of the size of the labor force can be made. For the major part of the model used in this study, a projection of the participation rate was not made for two reasons: First, because there is still a good deal of subsistence agriculture in Jamaica, it is difficult to ascertain whether or not a member

TABLE 8

Equivalent Adult Consumers, Jamaica, 1960-65
(In Thousands)

Weighted as follows:

Factor	Age Groups
0.35	0-4
0.50	5-9
0.75	10-14
1.00	15+

Age Groups	1960		1961		1962		1963		1964		1965	
	Population	Equivalent Adult Consumers	Population	Equivalent Adult Consumers	Population	Equivalent Adult Consumers	Population	Equivalent Adult Consumers	Population	Equivalent Adult Consumers	Population	Equivalent Adult Consumers
0-4	283.1	99.1	298.7	104.5	302.2	105.8	304.5	106.6	311.3	108.9	313.8	109.8
5-9	221.2	110.6	239.0	119.5	248.8	124.4	259.8	129.9	270.2	135.1	283.4	141.7
10-14	174.3	130.7	187.2	140.4	195.2	146.4	203.8	152.9	214.1	160.6	224.5	168.4
15+	949.6	949.6	921.3	921.3	913.6	913.6	928.4	928.4	944.2	944.2	966.5	966.5
All Ages	1,628.2	1,290.0	1,646.2	1,285.7	1,659.8	1,290.2	1,696.5	1,317.8	1,739.8	1,348.8	1,788.2	1,386.4
ΔN[a]				4.3		4.5		27.6		31.0		37.6

aIncrease in equivalent adult consumers.

of a farmer's household is in the labor force. Second, whether
or not a worker offers himself for paid employment is itself
a function of economic variables, such as the level of the real
wage. Thus, while objections could be raised to postulating
the same participation rate in the labor force for each fertility
projection over time, it may be even more inappropriate to
forecast the results of the comparisons by postulating different
participation rates.

    This problem of participation in the labor force has been
handled in other demographic-econometric studies by assuming
that all or some proportion of the population between certain
ages constitutes the labor force. In all these studies, the assumption is implicit that participation rates do not change
through time. To the extent that the assumption holds, the
proportionate changes in total population can serve as a surrogate for what the labor force might actually have been. For
simplicity, therefore, the contribution of labor to output in
this study is set equal to the mid-year estimate of the population between fifteen and sixty-four. This concept of labor
force will be used in all analyses, except the one dealing with
unemployment.

    As indicated above, projections of the working-age popula-
tion have been and can be used as a surrogate for labor force
given the assumption that participation rates do not change
materially through time. Changes in participation rates may,
admittedly, be hard to measure, and it may be improper to
predict what these changes might be. (There is an obvious
interaction between labor participation and output as well as
vice versa). But in countries where data are sufficiently good
to distinguish between employment and unemployment, some
improvement in calculating the contribution of labor to output
can, perhaps, be made.

    Stephen Enke, William McFarland, and others, in a re-
cent demographic-econometric model prepared for the United
States Agency for International Development (USAID), make
such a distinction. [5] They make no attempt to postulate any
changes in participation rates; their model simply seeks to
distinguish between available labor (L) and employed labor
(L').

    The Enke-McFarland model postulates that increasing
capital stock (K) not only raises output per worker but reduces
the surplus labor ratio (L/L'). The greater amount of capital
stock obtainable under low fertility rather than high fertility
has the effect of reducing the unemployment rate. The employment function takes the following form:

$$L_t' = \left(1 + g \frac{K_t - K_{t-1}}{K_{t-1}}\right) L_{t-1}'$$

where

$$g = h \left[\frac{L_{t-1} - L_{t-1/t-1}'}{L_o - L_o'/L_o}\right]$$

L' = Employed labor
K = Capital stock
L = Labor force
g = Proportionality coefficient
h = Employment function coefficient
o = Subscript indicating initial values.

How this function works is, perhaps, best explained in their own words:

> The percent increase in employed labor is some proportion, g, of the percent increase in the stock of capital. The proportion is determined by the unemployment rate and decreases from an initial value of h to a value of zero as the unemployment rate decreases from its initial value to zero.
> The coefficient h, is a parameter and has two roles. The first is to determine the initial rela-tionship between the growth rates of capital stock and employed labor. Initially, g = h. If h is larger than unity, employed labor initially grows more rapidly than the capital stock. If h has an initial value of unity, the unemployment rate will rise, fall, or remain constant, depending on whether the growth rate of capital is less than, greater than, or equal to the growth rate of the labor force.
> The second role of h is to determine the effect of a given change in the unemployment rate on the coefficient g. The larger h is, the larger will be the change in the proportionality coefficient g, which results from a given change in the rate of unemployment. Thus, it measures the sensitivity of the incremental capital-labor ratio to changes in the unemployment rate. In other words, the effects of an increase in h are (1) to increase the value of g for any given unemployment rate, and (2) to increase the sensitivity of g to changes in the unemployment rate. [6]

Thus, briefly, the change in employment is the ratio of
current unemployment to initial unemployment in base year
times h. This parameter h is a measure of the initial "labor
intensity" of output. It can be expressed as follows:

$$h = \frac{\Delta L' K}{L' \Delta K.}$$

A good deal of work was involved in trying to adapt this
concept for the Jamaican data. Estimates of employed labor
were constructed serially--that is, one year provided information for the successive year, and the years had to be calculated
in order. First, estimates of total labor force in the base
year of the model needed to be obtained. The last labor force
survey adequate for estimating participation rates was from
the 1960 Jamaican census.

Here some definitional problems arose. The classified
labor force in Jamaica includes only those who have previously
worked. Those seeking their first job (and they exceed those
who have previously worked and are unemployed) need to be
included to obtain a proper estimate of unemployment. When
job seekers are included, as in Table 9, unemployment rates
for male and female are substantially increased in the younger
age categories. [7]

Similarly, an adjustment had to be made for part-time
workers. The total work force in full-time equivalents was
equal to .95 of the total number employed. In Table 11, allowance for underemployment and for unemployment produces
an estimated unemployment rate of 13.7 percent.

The labor force participation rates for 1960 were used as
a constant throughout the projection period. The labor force
(L) for each year from 1967 to 2020 was estimated by multiplying these rates by the size of yearly age-sex population groups.
Unemployment for 1967 was set at 13 percent, a slight improvement over 1960. [8]

The estimates for employed labor, however, required a
determination of the value of h, the employment function coefficient. McFarland, the primary developer of the concept,
assumed that setting h equal to 1 was an equivalency suitable
for developed countries. He thought a value of .6 would be
appropriate for markedly underdeveloped countries, and of
.8 for semideveloped countries like Jamaica. [9]

To test the suitability of these values, proportionate
changes in the capital-labor ratio, assuming no changes in the

TABLE 9

Calculation of Labor Force and Participation Rates, Jamaica, 1960

	(a) Males			
Age Groups	Numbers Seeking First Job	Classified Labor Force	Total Labor Force	Participation Rates
10-14	898	1,402	2,300	2.647
15-19	14,298	39,128	53,426	77.994
20-24	3,614	51,343	54,957	96.416
25-34	723	89,910	90,633	97.770
35-44	-	78,814	78,814	97.301
45-54	-	68,697	68,697	95.413
55-64	-	36,689	36,689	87.355
65+	-	15,675	15,675	54.617
Total	19,533	381,658	401,191	

	(b) Females			
Age Groups	Numbers Seeking First Job	Classified Labor Force	Total Labor Force	Participation Rates
10-14	762	633	1,395	1.596
15-19	16,794	24,469	41,263	53.868
20-24	8,609	35,228	43,837	64.277
25-34	2,061	60,200	62,261	55.245
35-44	-	47,010	47,010	51.659
45-54	-	35,139	35,139	48.202
55-64	-	16,807	16,807	37.266
65+	-	5,679	5,679	13.784
Total	28,226	225,165	253,391	

Source: Jamaica Department of Statistics (O. C. Francis), The People of Modern Jamaica (Kingston, 1963), chaps. 7 and 8.

TABLE 10

Estimation of Unemployment, Jamaica, 1960

Labor Force	Total	Male	Female
Total labor force	654,582	401,191	253,391
Employed	566,451	363,371	203,080
Not seeking work	3,228	1,883	1,345
Unemployed	84,903	35,937	48,966
Percent Unemployment	13.0	9.0	19.3

Source: Jamaica Department of Statistics (O. C. Francis), The People of Modern Jamaica (Kingston, 1963); chaps. 7 and 8, Tables 7.1, 8.1, and 8.2.

TABLE 11

Adjustment for Unemployment, Jamaica, 1960

Underemployed	Number	Average Number of Days Worked	Number of Equivalent Work Days
Working one to two days	30,355	1.5	45,532.5
Working three to four days	115,098	3.5	402,843.0
Working five days or more	401,222	5.5	2,206,721.0
Ill	19,776	-	-

Full-time equivalent employed $\frac{2,655,096.5}{5} = 531,019$

Not seeking work   3,228

Unemployed   84,903

Percent Unemployment   13.7

Source: Jamaica Department of Statistics (O. C. Francis), The People of Modern Jamaica (Kingston, 1963), chaps. 7 and 8, Tables 7.1, 8.1, and 8.2

unemployment rate, were calculated for Jamaica over a fifty-
year period under high, medium, and low productivities of
capital and under varying fertility assumptions. As regards
the rate of growth of labor relative to the rate of growth of
capital, labor, in all cases, increased at a markedly lower
rate than capital. What this means is that for a given increase
in capital, the increase in employment will be less than proportional.

Proportionate changes in the capital-labor ratio ranged
from . 97, when the productivity of capital is low and fertility
is high, to . 34, when the productivity of capital is high and
the fertility is low.

These proportionate changes in capital-labor ratios were
calculated assuming no changes in the unemployment rate. In
the situation of continued economic growth, however, unemployment rates should decline. Thus the value of h would be
slightly less than the changes observed, since it is affected
by the relationship of current to initial unemployment rates.

Because the change from year-to-year in unemployment
rates is gradual and the values for h are an approximation,
the observed changes in capital-labor ratios have been employed without further modification. A single value of h for
all capital productivity and fertility assumptions is not valid,
however, and, based on observed changes in capital-labor
ratios, a series of values of h are used for the Jamaica projections, as indicated in Table 12.

Births Prevented and Acceptors

Because fertility reduction is not costless, estimates of
both births prevented and number of equivalent acceptors are
needed under various fertility assumptions over time. (The
constant high-fertility assumption is the exception in that no
births are prevented and no acceptors are involved.)

The number of births prevented is a function of the age
composition of females at a given period of time, the number
within each age group using effective contraceptive measures,
and the fertility that otherwise would have prevailed had these
acceptors not opted for birth control. For the sake of simplicity,
the fertility assumptions adopted in the Jamaica model postulates an equal percent decline for all age-specific birth rates
through time and that all such declines begin at the same time
interval for all fertility assumptions.

To calculate the number of births for each five-year

TABLE 12

Values of h, the Employment Function Coefficient

Fertility Assumption	Productivity of Capital			
	.3	.5	.7	1.0
High	.97	.95	.91	.75
Medium	.79	.75	.68	.48
Low	.68	.62	.54	.34

interval of this model, there are two ways in which the data can be handled. If, for example, the "medium" assumption is made that age-specific birth rates decline by 5 percent per five-year period, one method is to assume that 5 percent of females in the childbearing ages have zero-fertility rates. A second method, resulting in the same number of births, can be arrived at by considering that the fertility of the group as a whole is 95 percent of what respective age-fertility rates were previously. Thus, in generalized form:

$$ASBR^{ti} = (ASBR)^{to} (i) (d)$$

- to = Time in base year
- ti = Time at interval i
- i = Length of time interval
- d = Rate of decrease per year.

Births prevented are the differences in a given time period between births that occurred and births that otherwise would have occurred in the absence of family planning.

$$BP^{ti} = B^{t'1} - B^{ti}$$

- BP = Births prevented
- $B^{t'1}$ = Births in the absence of family planning
- B^{ti} = Births under reduction of fertility.

The number of births is a result of age-specific birth rates and the number of females of childbearing age in each respective population projection (under high, medium, low, and very low fertility assumptions). The number of births in the absence of family planning and the number of births in the presence of family planning under a given population projection, x, give an estimate of births prevented. Thus:

$$BP^{ti} = F_x^{ti} \left(ASBR_x^{to} - ASBR_x^{ti} \right)$$

F_x^{ti} = Number of females in childbearing ages under population projection based on fertility reduction assumption, x.

Births prevented are not the same as the number of those practicing effective contraception. If, for example, the age-specific fertility rate for a group of women is .2, there is one chance in five that a woman will give birth in that particular year. Put another way, five acceptors are needed, on the average, to prevent one birth. It can be thus seen that the number of births prevented is inversely related to the age-specific birth rates of the acceptors. The number of contraceptive acceptors needed to bring about a stipulated reduction in fertility rates can be expressed as:

$$A = F_x^{ti} \left(1 - \frac{ASBR_x^{ti}}{ASBR^{to}} \right)$$

or

$$F_x^{ti} \left[1 - i(d) \right]$$

The age-specific birth rates to which declines in fertility are related are the "otherwise" rates, which reflect the high fertility of the base-year time interval. The interpretation of the relationship between births prevented and acceptors of contraceptive practices is that, while the cost per acceptor is constant, the number of acceptors who must be reached where age-specific fertility rates are low is proportionately greater to achieve the same reduction in the number of births.

Separate calculations of both acceptors and births prevented have been computed for all fertility assumptions over time in the model.

Outline of Demographic Outputs

Direct demographic output for the projection period consists of:
1. Population, by age and sex
2. Equivalent adult consumers

3. Age groups
    a. Young dependents (ages zero to fourteen)
    b. Working age (ages fifteen to sixty-four)
    c. Old dependents (ages sixty-five and over)
4. Reduction in births resulting directly from decline in fertility
5. Number of contraceptive acceptors needed to bring about stipulated reductions in births.
    Derived values and ratios include:
1. Crude birth rate
2. Crude death rate
3. Dependency ratio
4. Age-sex profiles of the population
5. Ratio of equivalent adult consumers to total population
6. Ratio of labor force to total population.

NOTES

1. United Nations, Department of Economic and Social Affairs, Methods for Population Projections by Sex and Age, Manual III, Population Studies No. 25 (ST/SOA/Ser. A) (New York, 1956); Ansley J. Coale and Paul Demeny, Regional Model Life Tables (Princeton, N.J.: Princeton University Press, 1966).

2. See for example, United Nations, Economic Commission for Latin America, Human Resources of Central America, Panama and Mexico, 1950-1980, in Relation to Some Aspects of Economic Development (ST/TAO/K/LAT. 1) (New York, 1960).

3. Kingsley Davis, "Population Policy: Will Current Programs Succeed?," Science, 158 (November 10, 1967), pp. 730-39.

4. Peter Newman and R. H. Allen, Population Growth Rates and Economic Development in Nicaragua (Washington, D.C.: Robert R. Nathan Associates, Inc., 1967), p. 20.

5. Stephen Enke, "Birth Control for Economic Development," Science, 164 (May 16, 1969), pp. 798-802; Stephen Enke, Gen. Ed., and William E. McFarland et al., Description of the Economic Demographic Model (68TMP-119) (Santa

Barbara, Calif.: TEMPO, General Electric Center for Advanced Studies, 1969).

6. Enke and McFarland, op. cit., pp. 16-17.

7. Calculations were based on data analyzed by O. C. Francis in Jamaica Department of Statistics, The People of Jamaica (Kingston, 1963), especially chap. VII, "Labour Force, including Projections of the Labour Force by Age and Sex" and chap. VIII, "Persons Seeking Their First Jobs. "

8. Jamaica Department of Statistics, Employment and Earnings in Large Establishments, 1965 (Kingston, 1967).

9. As suggested to me by letter from William McFarland, June 5, 1969.

CHAPTER **3** THE MODEL:
ECONOMIC
RELATIONSHIPS

FEATURES INCLUDED IN THE MODEL

In constructing the model for studying the relations in
Jamaica between population growth and economic growth, one
needs to distinguish those economic factors or variables most
affected by fertility differences. Suggestions on what these
variables should be and on what assumptions underlie the
growth-model approach come from analysis of seven studies
cited in Chapter 1 (pages 10-11, notes 3 and 4). Table 12
indicates the ways in which the earlier studies have operated
suggestively and indicates, also, those factors that are unique
to this model.

Obviously, as was the case in all previous studies the
Jamaican study must measure (a) demand for private consumption, (b) demand for public consumption, and (c) supply
of capital funds or savings as affected by consumption demands.
Here, savings are calculated directly as a function of population and income rather than as a residual after the calculation
of consumption demands. In all models, the effect of population growth rates on consumption and/or savings (investment)
is the most important relationship examined. Similarly, the
Jamaican model, like the others, considers (d) the effects of
changes in the ratio of workers to consumers and (e) the effect
of changes in capital (investment) on output. This study, unlike
the three using the Harrod-Domar production function, ascribes
changes in output to changes in labor as well as capital.

This study, as are the four models using the Cobb-Douglas
production function, is concerned with (f) the effect of changes
in labor on output and (g) the effect of factor returns--that is,
the proportionate relationship between capital and labor.

Though less-often considered in other growth model studies, the following are of significance here: (h) the effect of
economies of scale on output, (i) costs of fertility reduction
programs, (j) costs of welfare investments, (k) foreign sector accounts, (l) savings as a function of total income,

39

TABLE 13

Studies Using the Growth-Model Approach

Feature of Model	Coale-Hoover[a]	Hoover-Perlman[a]	Demeny[a]	Newman-Allen[b]	Enke[b]	Lloyd[b]	Ruprecht[b]
1. Demand for Private Consumption	Y[c]	Y	Y	Y	Y	Y	Y
2. Demand for Public Consumption	Y	Y	Y	Y	P[d]	Y	Y
3. Supply of Capital as Affected by Consumption Demands	Y	Y	Y	Y	Y	Y	Y
4. Effect of Changes in the Ratio of Workers to Consumers	P	P	P	Y	Y	Y	Y
5. Effect of Changes of Capital on Output	Y	Y	Y	Y	Y	Y	Y
6. Effect of Changes of Labor on Output	P	N[e]	N	Y	Y	Y	Y
7. Effect of Factor Returns on Output	P	N	N	Y	N	N	N
8. Effect of Economies of Scale on Output	N	N	N	Y	P	N	P
9. Inclusion of Costs of Fertility Reduction Program	N	N	Y	N	Y	Y	N
10. Calculation of Costs of Welfare Investment	Y	Y	N	N	N	N	Y
11. Inclusion of Foreign Sector Accounts	N	P	N	Y	P	N	N
12. Savings Made Primarily a Function of Total Income	N	N	N	N	Y	Y	Y
13. Provision for Autonomous Growth	N	Y	Y	N	Y	Y	Y
14. Effect of Changes of Capital-Labor Ratio on Employment	N	N	N	N	Y	N	P

[a] This model employs the Harrod-Domar production function.
[b] This model employs the Cobb-Douglas production function.
[c] Y equals fully taken into account
[d] P equals substantially or partially taken into account
[e] N equals not considered in the study.

(m) provisions for autonomous growth, and (n) the effect in employment of changes in the capital-labor ratio.

The purpose of the model is to analyze the effects of varying levels of fertility on a number of economic variables. When these fertility assumptions are being contrasted, all other assumptions must be held constant. The structure of the model, the form of the equations, and the values of the productivities of capital and labor, savings rate, and rate of autonomous growth remain unchanged from one projection to another.

A basic limitation of the model--it must be stressed again-- is that the projections are not to be treated as forecasts. They illustrate what would happen if stated assumptions are satisfied over the projection period. Reasonable values for the parameters, based on time-series analysis, have been determined.

The model is highly aggregated, as are all the others used in demographic-econometric studies. Data generally available in developing countries are suitable for this degree of aggregation. Given the present state of knowledge about economic systems and the fact that aggregate relationships usually exhibit greater stability than the microrelationships of which they are composed, one can not feasibly consider using a lower level of aggregation.

ECONOMIC INPUTS OF THE MODEL

Data requirements for the economic part of the model are as follows:

1. Base year values (t-1) for gross national product, welfare investment, and government consumption
2. The initial stocks of fixed capital for first projection year, t, both total and productive only
3. Initial value for the arithmetic mean of gross national product for previous five years
4. The annual rate of technological change, when applicable
5. Coefficients of the production function for capital and labor, under varying productivities and returns to scale
6. The initial estimate of mid-year working age population for year t
7. Weights to be applied to different age groups in the population to compute the number of equivalent adult consumers
8. Average propensity to save prior to making allowance for

net additions to the population under high, medium, and low savings assumptions

9. Average cost per contraceptive acceptor.

When the model uses the labor force concept of available and employed labor, additional input data needed are the following:

10. A set of age- and sex-specific labor force participation rates by five-year cohorts

11. The initial rate of unemployment

12. The initial proportionality coefficient between the growth rates of capital stock and employed labor.

ECONOMIC OUTPUTS OF THE MODEL

Levels and rates of economic growth generated are the following: (a) gross national product; (b) capital stock, total and productive only; (c) private, public, and total consumption; (d) gross domestic savings; (e) net borrowing from abroad (foreign savings); (f) gross domestic investment; (g) fixed capital formation, total and productive only; (h) welfare investment; (i) demographic investment; (j) imports minus exports; and (k) net foreign transfer payments.

When using alternate concept of labor force, additional outputs are the following: (l) labor force; (m) employed labor; and (n) unemployed labor.

Ratios and values calculated are the following: (o) gross national product per equivalent adult consumer; (p) private, public, and total consumption per equivalent adult consumer; (q) capital-labor ratio; (r) ratio of investment to gross national product; (s) marginal product of capital; and (t) marginal product of labor.

STRUCTURE OF THE MODEL

To produce the economic inputs and outputs described above, it is necessary to derive the structure of the model. The structure described in the following pages is based on the features of the demographic-economic relationships considered important in this study and takes the form of a series of simultaneous equations.

Production Function

The technical conditions under which the various factors of production combine to produce outputs may be defined as the production function. This study uses the Cobb-Douglas production function, which allows for capital and labor each to contribute positively to output regardless of the level of the other factor.

The form of the production function used here is:

$$(1) \quad Y_t = aK_t^u L_t^v q^n$$

Y = Gross national product in year t

K = Stock of fixed productive capital at beginning of year

L = Mid-year working age population, fifteen to sixty-four

u = Exponent representing fractional share of gross national value added by capital

v = Exponent representing fractional share of gross national product value added by labor

a = Conversion coefficient relating capital-labor units to gross national product

q = Annual rate of technological progress

n = Years elapsed from base year.

Leaving aside, for the moment, the variant allowing for the influence of technological progress or autonomous growth, the Cobb-Douglas production function contains in simple, compact form most of the analytical characteristics relevant to demographic-econometric analysis. The function is linear and homogeneous; under constant returns to scale, the doubling of the quantities of both labor and capital will double the product.

Changes in Capital and Labor

The exponents of capital and labor, u and v, each have a simple interpretation. Assuming a productivity of capital (u = .3) and labor (v = .7) as illustrative, one notes that an increase in the stock of capital (K) by 1 percent with labor (L) constant would increase product (Y) by .3 percent. An increase in L of 1 percent, with K constant, would increase Y by .7 percent. An increase of both K and L by 1 percent would increase Y by 1 percent. In fact, both capital and labor increase together, though usually at different rates, and it is important to be able to distinguish the effects of each.

Factor Returns

The increase in total product caused by the addition of one more unit of capital declines as more capital is added and labor is kept fixed. Put another way, the marginal product of capital decreases with increases in capital, provided that the productivity of capital (u) is less than one. The smaller u is, the faster will be the rate of decrease of total product as capital is added; and the larger the capital stock is already, the faster will be the decline in the marginal product. Thus, the faster capital is accumulated with respect to labor, the less "efficient" is each additional unit of capital relative to labor. (Exactly the same statements hold with regard to labor and its productivity coefficient, v.) However, at all times, each factor contributes positively to product, provided that its coefficient (u or v) is greater than zero.

Returns to Scale

If capital and labor increase simultaneously, total product depends directly on the sum of the coefficients u and v. If (u + v) = 1, then product increases by the same percent as the increase in capital and labor (constant returns to scale). If (u + v) is greater than 1, for example, 1.1, there are increasing returns to scale, and product increases more than proportionately (in the example, 10 percent higher). If (u + v) is less than 1 (e.g., 0.9), there are decreasing returns to scale, and the product increases by 10 percent less than under constant returns to scale.

The coefficients u and v summarize the conditions of production. Their sum indicates how favorable production conditions are: the larger the sum, the more favorable the conditions, while the size of the individual coefficients reflects the "efficiency" of the corresponding factor. The two coefficients are especially relevant for varying fertility projections, where both factors are changing together but not in the same proportions. In such circumstances, the outcome will be the resultant of two effects: the "scale" effect of a change of both factors together and the effect of a change in the proportion of capital to labor, or the capital-labor ratio.

The model is not intended to pinpoint the single best set of assumptions of the productivities of capital and labor, but rather to offer a realistic range of conditions that could prevail in the future.

Capital, therefore, is considered under four levels of

TABLE 14

Capital and Labor Productivities Used in the Model

Levels of Capital Productivity	u	v	u + v	Returns to Scale
Low	0.3	0.6	0.9	Decreasing
	0.3	0.7	1.0	Constant
	0.3	0.8	1.1	Increasing
Medium	0.5	0.4	0.9	Decreasing
	0.5	0.5	1.0	Constant
	0.5	0.6	1.1	Increasing
High	0.7	0.2	0.9	Decreasing
	0.7	0.3	1.0	Increasing
	0.7	0.4	1.1	Constant
All Increases in Productivity Attributable to Capital	1.0	0.0	1.0	Constant

productivity: low, medium, high, and total (the Harrod-Domar concept). Except in the last case, in which the capital exponent is unity and labor zero, the other productivity exponents of capital are given representative values of .3, .5, and .7. These three levels of capital productivity (u) are then matched with appropriate levels of labor productivity (v) to give diminishing, constant, and increasing returns to scale. Schematically, this concept is represented in Table 14.

While no great significance attaches to the particular values of the exponents selected in the model, one can reasonably surmise that the importance of the contribution of capital will decrease over time and that in the long run, there is a probability of decreasing returns to scale for both labor and capital. What this difference might be will depend largely on demographic factors, but as the limit is approached to the total amount of natural resources or land available, diminishing returns to scale are likely to occur. The potential economies of scale that may be realized through larger markets and fuller utilization of social overhead may be more than offset by diminishing returns in terms of both increased economic costs of production and higher living costs due to concentrated urban growth.

Contributions to Output Other Than Labor and Capital

The most general way of handling the effect of technological progress on increasing production is to assign a term for it in the production function. Such progress can be considered a form of autonomous growth, and increases in productivity attributable to technology are considered to be about 2.5 percent a year in developed countries. As suggested by Enke, a rate of 1.5 percent is typical of underdeveloped countries, and this is the value adopted in this study. [1]

Technological progress will be regarded as neutral, equally saving of both labor and capital, and hence, not affecting their exponents. Because it is convenient to assume no innovations with which to begin, the Cobb-Douglas production function without provision for autonomous growth is used first in determining demographic-econometric relationships.

Measurement of Product

In the model, production is measured in terms of gross national product. This is, by far, the most widely used and most plausible in terms of relationships to other economic variables. To use the concept of domestic product is to include some product and income accruing to nonresidents, thus affecting both consumption and saving propensities. To measure product on a net basis (net of depreciation) has the apparent advantage of avoiding explicit consideration of depreciation in the model. However, because additions to capital stock from year to year are measured by changes in net investment, regardless of what concept of production is used, measuring product net of depreciation in no way removes the necessity of calculating depreciation to arrive at a figure for capital stock.

Capital Formation

Capital stock (K) is defined in the model as the stock of fixed productive capital at the beginning of the year. Depreciation, however, is calculated as a proportion of the total stock of fixed capital, both productive and nonproductive (K') at the beginning of the year. This broader concept of capital stock is also needed in the model so that the effect of welfare investment, considered here as not contributing to the further production of goods and services, can be properly taken into account.

The concept that capital stock comprises fixed productive capital only is the one used to determine the contribution of capital to product in the model. Additions of this kind of capital stock only generate increases in income and product. Thus if K represents the stock of fixed productive capital and K' represents the stock of all fixed capital, productive and nonproductive, the respective capital stock identities may be written:

$$(2) \quad K_t = K_{t-1} + J_{t-1}$$

$$(3) \quad K'_t = K'_{t-1} + J'_{t-1}$$

K = Stock of fixed productive capital at beginning of year
J = Net fixed productive capital formation
K' = Total stock of fixed capital, (productive and non-productive), at beginning of year
J' = Net fixed capital formation both productive and non-productive.

Given gross domestic investment (I), it is necessary to determine net fixed capital formation, both productive and nonproductive (J). Such determination involves netting out two factors: change in inventories and allowance for capital consumption. Although changes in inventory stock appear to increase during slowdowns in gross investment, the percent of gross investment going to increases in inventory has varied little over time.

This adjustment for inventory has been ignored in all but one other demographic-econometric growth model to date, but since it is a constant proportion, it does not affect the relationship of economic variables to various fertility assumptions.[2] It does, however, have an absolute effect to the extent that the estimated amount of productive investment becomes greater than it should be, with consequent further increase of the capital-labor ratio and decrease in the marginal productivity of capital. Gross investment net of inventory can be written:

$$I' = bI_t$$

I' = Gross investment net of inventory
b = Coefficient representing proportion of gross investment in fixed capital to total gross investment
I = Gross investment.

No number is assigned to this equation because it is not

separately solved in the model. The relationship is incorporated in (5), determination of net fixed capital formation.

The second adjustment is to net out depreciation--both
depreciation of existing capital stock and allowance for obso-
lescence in stock not otherwise depreciated. The process is
necessary to the estimation of net fixed capital formation,
both productive and nonproductive. Depreciation is, therefore,
calculated as a percent of all capital stock. The capital consumption allowance is:

$$(4) \quad D_t = dK'_t$$

D = Capital consumption allowance
d = Coefficient representing capital consumption as
    percent of capital stock
K' = Stock of fixed capital both productive and nonproductive,
    at beginning of year.

Net fixed capital formation, productive and nonproductive,
is expressed as:

$$(5) \quad J'_t = bI_t - D_t$$

J' = Net investment in fixed capital, productive and non-
    productive
b = Coefficient representing proportion of gross invest-
    ment in fixed capital to total gross investment
I = Gross investment
D = Capital consumption allowance.

The next step in the process is to estimate the formation of
net fixed productive capital. From any given net investment in
overall fixed capital, there must be netted out two types of investment that are not productive in the sense of directly gen-
erating output. The first of these is welfare investment, defined here as ownership of dwellings (from the private sector)
plus government investment in fixed capital facilities in social
services and community services of health, education, public
housing, and other welfare.

The cost of welfare investment in the model is stated as:

$$(6) \quad WI_t = WI_{t-1} \left(\frac{gc_t}{gc_{t-1}} \right) + wi_t \Delta N$$

WI = Welfare investment
gc = Government consumption per equivalent adult consumer
wi = Welfare investment per equivalent adult consumer
ΔN = Increase from previous year of equivalent adult consume

The concept involved is that welfare investment in a given year is considered to be equal to the previous year's outlay multiplied by the ratio of government consumption for the current year to the previous year, plus provision of welfare services at current levels for additions to the population.

In arriving at an estimate of fixed capital formation, provision is made for costs of a program of fertility reduction. Such costs are called here "demographic investment" and constitute a separate, additional type of investment, which, like welfare investment, is considered as not making a direct contribution to output. The most conservative assumption is made; all expenditures for fertility reduction are at the expense of resources that would otherwise be used for investment to increase output.

The cost per acceptor of contraceptive methods is an averaged cost of both new and old acceptors. Certain contraceptive methods involve a higher initial cost with lower continuation costs, whereas other methods may have proportionately higher continuation costs because of the need of resupplying contraceptive materials. Rather than attempting a differential cost of new acceptors at a certain amount and of previous acceptors at, perhaps, half that amount, it is simpler and clearer to estimate demographic investment on the basis of an average figure, representing a mix of all acceptors and contraceptive methods, including prorated costs of salaries, overhead, and educational programs. This relationship can be written as:

$$(7) \quad DI_t = A_t \, (c)$$

DI = Demographic investment
A = Number of acceptors of contraceptive methods
c = Average cost per contraceptive acceptor.

An estimate of cost per acceptor, however, does not represent the cost per prevented birth. Since most demographic-econometric studies center upon the value of a prevented birth, this value will be employed in the sections dealing with an analysis of the results of this mode.

Having separately determined welfare investment and demographic investment, one calculates net fixed productive capital formation as:

$$(8) \quad J_t = J'_t - WI_t\left(\frac{bI_t}{J'_t}\right) - DI_t$$

J = Net fixed productive capital formation
J' = Net fixed capital formation, both productive and non-productive

WI = Welfare investment
bI = Gross investment net of inventory
DI = Demographic investment.

Savings and Investment

The gross investment in any period is financed by both domestic savings and foreign savings. The latter represents net borrowing from abroad and is defined as the deficit on the current account of the balance of payments. The savings investment identity is:

$$(9) \quad I_t = B_t + E_t$$

I = Gross investment
B = Gross domestic savings
E = Net borrowing from abroad.

The domestic savings function used here includes personal, business, and public savings. Following the suggestion of Myrdal, savings are made a function of total income only rather than income per head.[3]

In the calculation of savings, allowance is made for increases in both private and public consumption to meet the needs of additions to the population. The savings function used implies that domestic saving increases with gross national product but is diminished by net additions to the population.

$$(10) \quad B_t = eY_t - gc_t \Delta N - pc_t \Delta N$$

B = Gross domestic savings
e = Average propensity to save, prior to making allowance for increases in government and private consumption for net additions to the population
gc = Government consumption per equivalent adult consumer
ΔN = Increase from pervious year of equivalent adult consumers
pc = Private consumption per equivalent adult consumer.

The definition of e, the average propensity to save, requires some additional explanation. Most growth models use the concept of marginal propensity to save (proportion saved out of increases of income) rather than average propensity to save (proportion of savings to total income). Generally, changes in savings relative to changes in income are rather volatile in year-to-year fluctuations. If, however, marginal and average propensities to save are close enough to be considered equal, then the latter approach of using average propensity to save would be indicated.

The coefficient e has a meaning beyond the average propensity to save. It can best be thought of in terms of its complementary consumption coefficient (1-e). If a reasonable value for e is .20, then (1-e) is .80. Of an increase of £J10 million in national income, 8 million of this rise will go to increasing the consumption (private and public) of a population the size of last year's. But because there will have been a net increase in the population since last year (measured in equivalent adult consumers), not all of the remaining £J2 million can go into actual saving. These additions to the population have a prior claim on the nation's resources before any saving can be done, in the sense that such additional persons must be provided food, clothing, and shelter, as well as public services.

A distinction is made in this study as to the types of increases in consumption expenditures. One type is the consumption-deepening component, which results from higher levels of income being made available for such purposes. The second type, the consumption-widening component, reflects increases in consumption to meet needs of additional population and is the only consumption component to have an effect on the propensity to save.

The logic of this assumption can be demonstrated by a simple example. In year 1, in Country X, from a national income of £J160 million, total consumption is £J128 million. Average propensity to consume is .8. In year 2, there is an increase of £J10 million, raising national income to £J170 million, of which £J8 million go for increasing consumption to a level of £J136 million. (As in most demographic-econometric studies, average and marginal propensities to consume are considered equal.) For the given population, N, per capita consumption has risen from 128 million/N to 136 million/N. This can be considered "deepening" in the sense that per capita consumption has increased, although the propensity to consume remains constant and, thus, also, the propensity to save.

Consumption-widening expenditures, however, do affect the propensity to save. Because there is no evidence otherwise that persons desire to lower their consumption standards or directly forego an increase in such levels, in order to take

care of additions to the population, an increase in population
normally postulates an increase in consumption at existing
levels. While, for certain families, this may imply a lowering of the levels of consumption for existing members, it will
be argued here that, in general, this is not the case. Aside
from whether the effects of the expenses of an additional member of a family are realistically perceived, most families in
underdeveloped countries are living at, or near, the subsistence level, and it would be very difficult, if not impossible,
to reduce further their already very low levels of consumption.

     To recapitulate--consumption levels of the existing popu-
lation (consumption deepening) are the results of given propensities to consume and do _not_ affect the amount of savings
available for investment. However, increases in consumption
to meet needs of additions to population (consumption widening)
require consumption expenditures in excess of those generated
by the given propensity to consume and, thereby, decrease
the amount of savings available for investment. This is
schematically represented in the following figure for increases
in private consumption; the illustration for government consumption would be identical.

FIGURE 1

**Widening and Deepening Components
of Consumption**

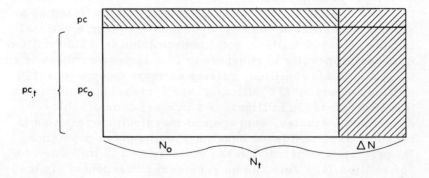

Private consumption in base year: Consumption widen-
$$PC_o = pc_o N_o$$ ing component

Private consumption in year t: Consumption deepen-
$$PC_t = pc_t N_t$$ ing component

Consumption deepening component = $\Delta pc\ N_o$
Consumption widening component = $pc_t \Delta N$

Having viewed the average propensity to save in terms of the propensity to consume, one can state that the savings co-efficient, e, is the average propensity to save prior to making allowance for increases in private and government consumption for net additions to the population. This value, naturally, will be greater than the observed propensity to save.

It is necessary in the savings function to compute both public and private consumption per adult consumer. This computation is made through a series of equations as follows:

$$(11)\ \ GC_t = GC_{t-1} + h\ \left(Y_t - Y_{t-1}\right)$$

GC = Government consumption
h = Marginal propensity of government consumption
Y = Gross national product.

This equation postulates that government consumption for a given year, t, is equal to the government consumption for the previous year, t-1, plus the product of the marginal propensity to consume, h, and the increase in gross national product from the previous year to the current year.

Government consumption per equivalent adult consumer by definition is:

$$(12)\ \ gc_t = \frac{GC_t}{N_t}$$

gc = Government consumption per equivalent adult consumer
GC = Government consumption
N = Mid-year adult consumers.

Private consumption is derived by solving three simultaneous equations: the savings-investment identity ($I_t = B_t + E_t$), the savings function ($B_t = eY_t - gc_t \Delta N - pc_t \Delta N$), and the national product-expenditure identity

$$(Y_t = PC_t + I_t + (X_t - M_t)0.$$

Y = Gross national product
PC = Private consumption
GC = Government consumption

I = Gross investment

(X-M) = Exports minus imports.

This gives us a function for estimating private consumption in a given year as:

$$(13) \quad PC_t = \frac{N_t}{N_{t-1}} \left(Y_t - GC_t - (X_t - M_t) \right) - E_t - eY_t + gc_t \Delta N^*$$

Again, by definition, private consumption per equivalent adult consumer is:

$$(14) \quad pc_t = \frac{PC_t}{N_t}$$

pc = Private consumption per equivalent adult consumer
PC = Private consumption
N = Mid-year equivalent adult consumers.

To complete the consumption function in the model, total consumption and total consumption per equivalent adult consumer are given by:

$$(15) \quad TC_t = PC_t + GC_t$$

TC - Total consumption
PC = Private consumption
GC = Government consumption.

$$(16) \quad tc_t = pc_t + gc_t$$

tc = Total consumption per equivalent adult consumer
pc = Total private consumption per equivalent adult consumer
gc = Total government consumption per equivalent adult consumer.

_____

*The three simultaneous equations are solved as follows:

$$(1) \quad Y_t = PC_t + GC_t + I_t + (X_t - M_t)$$
or
$$PC_t + I_t = Y_t - GC_t - (X_t - M_t)$$

$$(2) \quad I_t = B_t + E_t$$
or
$$I_t - B_t = E_t$$

$$(3) \quad B_t = eY_t - gc_t \Delta N - pc_t \Delta N$$
or
$$B_t + pc_t \Delta N = eY_t - gc_t \Delta N$$

The other part of the savings investment identity is concerned with E, net borrowing from abroad (equation 9). This supply of foreign saving is very difficult to project and is calculated simply as a constant fraction of the gross national product, Y, of the previous five years.

$$(17)\ \ E_t = f\overline{Y}_t$$

E = Net borrowing from abroad
f = Coefficient representing proportion of net borrowing from abroad to arithmetic mean of previous five years gross national product
$\overline{Y}$ = Arithmetic mean of previous five years gross national product.

G, net foreign transfer payments, is calculated on exactly the same basis.

$$(18)\ \ G_t = g\overline{Y}t$$

G = Net foreign transfer payments
g = Coefficient representing proportion of net borrowing from abroad to arithmetic mean of previous five years gross national product
$\overline{Y}$ = Arithmetic mean of previous five years gross national product.

Thus   (2) $I_t - B_t = E_t$

   + (3) $pc_t \Delta N + B_t = e Y_t - gc_t \Delta N$

   = (4) $I_t + pc_t \Delta N = E_t + e Y_t - gc_t \Delta N$

   - (1) $I_t + PC_t = Y_t - GC_t - (X_t - M_t)$

   = (5) $pc_t \Delta N - PC_t = E_t + e Y_t - gc_t \Delta N - Y_t + GC_t + (X_t - M_t)$

or $PC_t - pc_t \Delta N = Y_t - GC_t - (X_t - M_t) - E_t - e Y_t + gc_t \Delta N$

$$PC_t - \frac{PC_t \Delta N}{N_t} = Y_t - GC_t - (X_t - M_t) - E_t - e Y_t + gc_t \Delta N$$

$$PC_t (N_t - \Delta N) = (Y_t - GC_t - (X_t - M_t) - E_t - e Y_t + gc_t \Delta N)\ N_t$$

$$\therefore PC_t = \frac{N_t}{N_{t-1}}\ (Y_t - GC_t - (X_t - M_t) - E_t - e Y_t + gc_t \Delta N)$$

Given the means to determine E and G, the balance of payments identity now gives us a value for imports minus exports (M-X).

$$(19) \quad E_t = (M_t - X_t) - G_t$$

E = Net borrowing from abroad
(M-X) = Imports minus exports
G = Net foreign transfer payments.

To know the value of (M-X) is necessary so that it can be placed in the national product-expenditure identity in solving private consumption, which, in turn, determines domestic saving. Since both E and G are derived by mechanical projections, however, little value can be placed on the estimates of (M-X) for purposes of projection.

A final part of the economic growth model of Jamaica, although not needed for the internal calculations, is the capital-labor ratio. This is a measure of capital stock per worker and can also be used as an indicator of the amount of investment necessary to provide work for one man. The capital-labor ratio is defined as:

$$(20) \quad r_t = \frac{K_t}{L_t}$$

r = Capital-labor ratio
K = Stock of fixed productive capital at beginning of year
L = Estimate of mid-year working age population.

THE WORKING OF THE MODEL

Up to this point, the structure for both the demographic and economic parts of the model has been discussed. The demographic part is self-operative, once certain base data and demographic relationships are included. The economic part of the model is somewhat more complicated to get functioning, because it depends on certain demographic outputs and on obtaining a number of parameters, which are employed in the twenty equations describing the economic relationships of the model.

What the model basically seeks to demonstrate are the effects of varying fertility in Jamaica on a number of economic

indices over a fifty-year projection period. The economic
structure consists of only those variables that can be considered as systematically related to changes in population
growth. Economic progress is measured by various indices,
such as per capita product (income), per capita consumption,
stock of fixed capital, savings, net fixed productive capital
formation, and employment.

It may be useful, therefore, to outline the structure of
the economic part of the model, indicate the demographic variables needed as inputs, and proceed to the steps involved in
solving the model.

Notation

Capital letters denote aggregate variables, and lower case
letters denote per capita indices and parameters. The subscript t designates the value of a variable at the end of year t
if it is a stock variable and during the period t if it is a flow
variable.

1 Economic variables (All are measured in 1960 constant
prices in thousands of Jamaican pounds. Per capita indices
in lower-case letters carry values in Jamaican pounds.)

   B = Gross domestic savings
   D = Capital consumption allowance
  DI = Demographic investment
   E = Net borrowing from abroad (foreign savings)
   G = Net foreign transfer payments
  GC = Government consumption
   I = Gross domestic investment
   J = Net fixed productive capital formation
  J' = Net fixed capital formation, both productive and non-
       productive
   K = Stock of fixed productive capital at beginning of year
  K' = Stock of fixed capital, both productive and nonproductive,
       at beginning of year
 M-X = Imports minus exports
  PC = Private consumption
  TC = Total consumption
  WI = Welfare investment
   Y = Gross national product
   $\overline{Y}$ = Arithmetic mean of previous five years gross national
       product
  gc = Government consumption per capita
  pc = Private consumption per capita

r = Capital-labor ratio

tc = Total consumption per capita

wi = Welfare investment per equivalent adult consumer.

2 Demographic variables

A = Number of contraceptive acceptors

L = Mid-year working age population, fifteen to sixty-four (or when using alternate concept involving employment function, total labor force)

L' = Employed labor

N = Mid-year equivalent adult consumers.

3 Parameters

a = Conversion constant in production function relating capital-labor units to gross national product

b = Coefficient representing proportion of gross investment in fixed capital to total gross domestic investment

c = Average cost per contraceptive acceptor

d = Coefficient representing capital consumption as percent of capital stock

e = Average propensity to save without allowance for increases in government and private consumption for net additions to the population

f = Coefficient representing proportion of net borrowing from abroad to arithmetic mean of previous five years gross national product

g = Coefficient representing proportion of net foreign transfer payments to arithmetic mean of previous five years gross national product

h = Marginal propensity of government consumption

n = Years elapsed from base year

q = Annual rate of technological progress

u = Exponent representing fractional share of gross national product value added by capital

v = Exponent representing fractional share of gross national product value added by labor.

Equations

Production function:

$$(1) \quad Y_t = a K_t^u L_t^v q^n$$

Capital accumulation identity of fixed productive capital:

$$(2) \quad K_t = K_{t-1} + J_{t-1}$$

Capital accumulation identity of fixed capital, both productive and nonproductive:

$$(3) \quad K'_t = K'_{t-1} + J'_{t-1}$$

Capital consumption allowance:

$$(4) \quad D_t = dK'_t$$

Net fixed capital formation:

$$(5) \quad J'_t = bI_t - D_t$$

Welfare investment:

$$(6) \quad WI_t = WI_{t-1} \left(\frac{gc_t}{gc_{t-1}} \right) + wi_t \Delta N$$

Demographic investment:

$$(7) \quad DI_t = A_t(c)$$

Net fixed productive capital formation:

$$(8) \quad J_t = J'_t - WI_t \left(\frac{bI_t}{J'_t} \right) - DI_t$$

Savings investment identity:

$$(9) \quad I_t = B_t + E_t$$

Savings function:

$$(10) \quad B_t = eY_t - gc_t \Delta N - pc_t \Delta N$$

Government consumption:

$$(11) \quad GC_t = GC_{t-1} + h(Y_t - Y_{t-1})$$

Government consumption per capita:

$$(12) \quad gc_t = \frac{GC_t}{N_t}$$

Private consumption:

$$(13) \quad PC_t = \frac{N_t}{N_{t-1}} (Y_t - GC_t - (X_t - M_t) - E_t - eY_t + gc_t \Delta N)$$

Private consumption per capita:

$$(14) \quad pc_t = \frac{PC_t}{N_t}$$

Total consumption:

$$(15) \quad TC_t = PC_t + GC_t$$

Total consumption per capita:

$$(16) \quad tc_t = pc_t + gc_t$$

Projection function for net borrowing from abroad:

$$(17) \quad E_t = f\overline{Y}_t$$

Projection function for net transfer payments:

$$(18) \quad G_t = g\overline{Y}_t$$

Balance of payments identity:

$$(19) \quad E_t = (M_t - X_t) - G_t$$

Capital-labor ratio:

$$(20) \quad r_t = \frac{K_t}{L_t}$$

The model contains twenty equations, shown above, which are solved to obtain estimates of the twenty economic variables: B, D, DI, E, G, GC, I, J, J', K, K', (M-X), PC, TC, WI, Y, gc, pc, tc, and r.

There are three demographic variables: A, L, and N, with a fourth variable L' used with the employed labor variant. Parameters that are assumed to vary from projection to projection are e, u, and v.

Steps in Solving the Model

Step 1. Select values for the parameters e, u, and v, and choose one of the fertility projections, starting with the high assumption.

Step 2. Compute the parameter a in the production function based on the value of Y_{t-1}. (This is the conversion constant relating capital-labor units to gross national product.) This estimate of a is valid for all years of the projection.

Step 3. Compute Y_t from production function, using initial estimate of K_t (Equation 1)

Thereafter, economic variables are solved in the following order:

Step 4.	E_t	(Equation 17)
Step 5.	G_t	(Equation 18)
Step 6.	$(M_t - X_t)$	(Equation 19)
Step 7.	r_t	(Equation 20)
Step 8.	GC_t	(Equation 11)
Step 9.	gc_t	(Equation 12)
Step 10.	PC_t	(Equation 13)
Step 11.	pc_t	(Equation 14)
Step 12.	TC_t	(Equation 15)
Step 13.	tc_t	(Equation 16)
Step 14.	B_t	(Equation 10)
Step 15.	I_t	(Equation 9)
Step 16.	D_t	(Equation 4)
Step 17.	J'_t	(Equation 5)
Step 18.	WI_t	(Equation 6)
Step 19.	DI_t	(Equation 7)
Step 20.	J_t	(Equation 8)

After Step 20, when the value of net fixed productive capital formation (J_t) is determined, the cycle can be repeated for subsequent years through 2020. Net fixed productive capital formation (J) is added to productive capital stock (K) at the beginning of the year to determine the amount of productive capital stock at the end of the year. This value of K at end of year, t-1, then becomes the value of K at the start of year t. The value of total productive stock (K') is determined in exactly the same manner by net additions to total fixed capital formation.

Economic outputs are generated under each of the four fertility assumptions. There are also four assumptions of capital productivity (.3, .5, .7, and 1.0) with corresponding values of labor productivity. Except when all increases in production are attributed to the contribution of capital, values in labor productivity are varied to reflect decreasing, constant, and increasing returns to scale. Up to this point, there are four times ten or forty combinations of factors. Add to these three variations in assumed saving propensities of .18, .20,

and .22, and the total number of combinations reaches 120.
If provision for autonomous growth is included, the total is
doubled to 240.   The alternate concept of labor force to measure changes in employment caused by changes in the capital-
labor ratio again doubles the number of combinations, and it
becomes readily apparent why some of these variations have
been curtailed after initially establishing consistency of results.

     To handle this mass of data, the computer is clearly in-
dicated.   In addition to the component to produce needed demographic output, all of the economic relationships described
have been programmed for the IBM 360 computer.   It was
necessary as a test check to solve the first year or two of the
projection period by hand calculation to ensure that the computer model was internally consistent and producing reasonable values.

                              NOTES

     1.   Stephen Enke and Richard G. Zind, "Effect of Fewer
Births on Average Income," Journal of Biosocial Sciences,
I, 1 (1969), 42.   Originally published by Enke as Raising Per
Capita Income Through Fewer Births (Santa Barbara, Calif.:
TEMPO, General Electric Center for Advanced Studies, 1967).

     2.   Theodore K. Ruprecht, "Fertility Control, Investment
and Per Capita Output: A Demographic Econometric Model of
the Philippines," Contributed Papers, International Union for
the Scientific Study of Population, Sydney Conference, August
21-25, 1967, pp. 98-107.

     3.   Gunnar Myrdal, Asian Drama (3 vols.: New York:
Pantheon Books Division of Random House, 1968), III, pp.
2073-74.

4

The previous two chapters have described the demographic and economic relationships of the model and the steps involved in its solution.   The problem still to be discussed is the matter of obtaining and treating certain kinds of data needed as inputs for the model.

The demographic inputs, given the age-sex composition of the base-year population, are all derived data.   The assumptions made about changes in fertility are reflected in changes in age-specific birth rates.   The single best assumption of future mortality experience permits derivation of survival rates over time.   With the addition of an assumed constant sex ratio at birth, all demographic outputs for the projection period can be generated.

The demographic data thus produced are combined with certain kinds of needed economic data.   Not all of these economic data are directly available, however, and certain additional procedures must be followed to obtain them.   Also needed is the calculation of values for parameters included in the structure of the model, utilizing time series analysis.   How these particular parameters and types of economic data were derived is described in the following pages.

CONSTANT PRICE INDEX

All economic variables used in the projections must be measured on a constant price basis in order to avoid fictitious changes in the value of money through inflation.   All variables are measured in terms of 1960 prices, since this is the base year used for planning by the Jamaican government.

Statistical data for Jamaica are relatively reliable, but much of the improvement is of recent origin.   The use of national income and product accounts employing the U. N.

system began in 1956 and marked some improvement over the
previous system. The estimates produced were less than
satisfactory. Following a two-year study, published in 1965,
income and product accounts were officially revised back to
1959. Largely because there had been some double-counting
of intermediate product appearing as final product, as a comparison of both the earlier and revised estimates for over-
lapping years reveals, the earlier figures for total product
have been overestimated by 5.89 percent.

In constructing an extended constant price index, a further
complication is that data from 1938 through 1955 are given in
1950 prices; data from 1953 through 1961, in 1956 prices; and
data from 1959 through 1966, in 1960 prices. Through 1953,
production by sector is given only at factor cost. The agriculture sector, which also included forestry and fishing, was,
until 1953, combined with mining. At some length, taking into
account some definitional differences, it was possible to construct an overall, implicit price deflator on a 1960 scale, but
only for the years 1953 through 1966.

From 1959 onward, the Department of Statistics of Jamaica
also constructed implicit price deflators for major components
of the economy, such as personal consumption, government
consumption, gross domestic investment, exports, imports,
gross national product, and national income. For calculations
of capital stock, fixed capital formation, and capital consumption allowance, the constant-price adjustment factor for gross
domestic investment was used. For calculations of other
variables, which involve more than one major component of
the economy, the price deflator for national income was employed. Unfortunately, use of different price deflators causes
income components to be nonadditive in constant price terms
(i.e., the total may be greater or less than the sum of the
parts).

The value of most parameters is based on data of 1959
through 1966. This is a short period for a time series, and
although attempts were made to employ data at least back to
1953, the shorter time-interval was opted for four reasons:
(a) all product and income accounts are revised to net out
double counting of intermediate product, (b) specific implicit
price deflators are available for major components only for
this time, (c) definitional differences arise in certain accounts
in the earlier years, and (d) the most recent economic relationships are more likely to prevail in the future, particularly
when a country has been experiencing very rapid economic
growth as has Jamaica.

TABLE 15

Gross National Product, Jamaica, 1959-66
(In Thousands of Jamaican Pounds)

Year	Gross National Product (Current Prices)	Price Deflator	Inverse[a]	Gross National Product (1960 Constant Prices)
1959	210, 175	97. 7	102. 35	215, 096
1960	227, 258	100. 0	100. 00	227, 258
1961	242, 731	104. 5	95. 69	232, 387
1962	253, 463	106. 7	93. 53	237, 492
1963	270, 116	110. 0	90. 91	245, 661
1964	294, 486	108. 8	91. 91	267, 890
1965	318, 682	111. 6	89. 61	286, 037
1966	339, 199	115. 6	86. 42	293, 483

[a]The adjustment factor is inversely related to the degree of inflation or deflation present.

Source: Jamaica Department of Statistics, National Income and Product, 1967, Account I (Kingston, April, 1968).

A measure of the growth of gross national product in both current and constant prices is given in Table 15.

It may be useful to describe how the numerical coefficients and parameters used in the various equations were calculated using Jamaican data. The values obtained and many of the methodological problems in getting them are representative of developing countries.

CAPITAL STOCK

There has been no previous estimate made for Jamaica of total capital stock. The closest attempt was a government study to determine fixed assets at the beginning of 1960 for the mining, manufacturing, and construction sectors. [1] Using this government study as a base, a reasonable estimate of capital stock for the economy as a whole was made. Fixed capital formation for the three sectors was computed as a percent of

all sectors. To avoid single-year irregularities, net investment in these three sectors to total investment was computed
for 1959 through 1961, giving an average value of 24.35 percent. [2] The estimate of fixed capital assets of the total economy
for the beginning of 1960 was then made by multiplying the value
of the assets of the three sectors by the reciprocal of their
proportion to the total (4.107). Calculations are shown in Table
16.

The capital stock figure shown for a given year is the
capital stock at the beginning of that year. Given an estimate
of total capital stock for 1960, subsequent year values were
calculated as follows.

First, adjusted gross domestic investment (I) for the years
1959 through 1966 was converted to 1960 constant prices in
Table 17 by using the price deflator for the gross investment
sector.

Second, gross domestic investment (I) was netted of inventory change in order to determine gross fixed capital formation. This is represented by the ratio b of gross fixed capital
formation to gross domestic investment and gives a value of
.94. This means that, on average, 6 percent of gross domestic
investment in a given year goes into net inventory accumulation
rather than to formation of fixed capital investment, as is indicated in Table 18.

Third, capital consumption allowance (D) was subtracted
from gross fixed capital formation (I) to obtain net fixed capital
formation J'. In Table 19, the net fixed capital formation for
each year was added to the capital stock figure for that year
(K'_t) to give the estimate of capital stock for the beginning of
the subsequent year (K'_{t+1}).

A check on the reasonableness of these capital stock estimates involved computing the rate of depreciation for each of
the years from 1959 through 1966. As a proportion of fixed
capital stock, the rate of depreciation appeared to be exceptionally stable, with neither an upward or downward trend and
with a value closely approximating 4 percent a year. If the
1960 base-year estimate of capital stock had been too high or
too low, the rate of depreciation for subsequent years would
have shown an irregular trend, as is shown in Table 20.

The adequacy of the capital stock estimates were further
tested by computing average and incremental capital-output
ratios. Average capital-output ratio for the period 1959 through
1966 is 2.7 The incremental capital-output ratio (ICOR) for the
same period is 4.2. The ICOR is solved by use of two equations:
(a) $Y_t = Y_0 (1 + r)^n$ to solve for r (equal to .045) and (b) $I_t = kr Y_t$.

TABLE 16

Estimate of Total Stock of Fixed Capital, Jamaica, 1960
(Current Values--In Thousands of Jamaican Pounds)

Sector	Gross Fixed Capital Formation[a]			Fixed Assets[b] 1960
	1959	1960	1961	
1. Mining	1,552	1,492	1,317	43,936.0
2. Manufacturing	7,719	7,555	8,959	40,412.6
3. Construction	2,044	2,167	2,196	2,760.8
Total-- 3 Sectors	11,315	11,214	12,472	87,109.4
4. Gross Fixed Capital Formation	45,400	49,600	48,900	
5. $\frac{1 + 2 + 3}{4}$(Percent)	24.92	22.61	25.51	Average = 24.35 Percent[c]

[a]From first source cited below.
[b]From second source cited below
[c]Fixed assets of three sectors as average of all sectors equals 24.35 percent
87,109.4 x 4.107 = £J 357,758 estimate of fixed assets for all sectors, 1960.

Sources: Jamaica Department of Statistics, National Income and Product, 1967, Table I. (Kingston, April, 1968); Jamaica Department of Statistics, Industrial Activity, Mining, Manufacture, Construction, 1960 (Kingston, February, 1963).

TABLE 17

Conversion of Gross Domestic Investment from Current
to 1960 Constant Prices, Jamaica, 1959-66
(In Thousands of Jamaican Pounds)

Year	Unadjusted Gross Domestic Investment	-Statistical= Discrepancy	Adjusted Gross Domestic Investment	Price Deflator	Inverse	Gross Domestic Investment (In 1960 Constant Prices)
1959	50,464	+342	50,122	105.4	94.88	47,561
1960	50,669	-1,219	51,888	100.0	100.00	51,888
1961	51,133	-1,896	53,029	110.0	90.91	48,195
1962	50,154	-1,816	51,970	115.0	86.96	45,187
1963	49,312	-543	49,855	112.5	88.89	44,304
1964	60,640	+210	60,430	115.5	86.58	52,326
1965	65,255	+742	64,513	114.6	87.26	56,307
1966	76,780	+995	75,785	124.4	80.39	60,923

Source: Adapted from Jamaica Department of Statistics, National Income and Product, 1967,
Account V (Kingston, April, 1968).

TABLE 18

Calculation of Gross Fixed Capital Formation
as Percent of Gross Domestic Investment,
Jamaica, 1959-66
(1960 Constant Prices--In Thousands
of Jamaican Pounds)

Year	Gross Domestic Investment - (I)	Inventory = Change	Gross Fixed Capital Formation	b
1959	47,561	5,524	42,037	.8839
1960	51,888	2,288	49,600	.9789
1961	48,195	3,333	44,862	.9308
1962	45,187	2,491	42,696	.9449
1963	44,304	3,411	40,893	.9230
1964	52,326	3,291	49,035	.9371
1965	56,307	1,833	54,474	.9674
1966	60,923	2,523	58,400	.9586

$$b = .9406$$
$$= .94$$

Source: Jamaica Department of Statistics, National Income and Product, 1967, Account V (Kingston, April, 1968).

NET PRODUCTIVE CAPITAL FORMATION

Thus far, discussion has been devoted to estimates of the total stock of fixed capital, both productive and nonproductive, K'. Since output is generated only by the former, it is necessary to separate out estimates of productive capital stock, K.

By definition, nonproductive capital stock is that used for welfare investment and demographic investment. Since, at present, outlays for the latter are negligible, the initial concern is to net out welfare investment in arriving at estimates of productive capital stock.

Welfare investment, as used here, represents outlays for private dwellings plus public expenditures of fixed capital for welfare purposes. (There are other welfare outlays, such as

TABLE 19

Calculation of Net Fixed Capital Formation
and Total Capital Stock, Jamaica, 1959-66
(1960 Constant Prices--In Thousands
of Jamaican Pounds)

Year	Gross Fixed Capital Formation -	Capital Consumption Allowance =	Net Fixed Capital Formation (J')	Total Capital Stock (K')
1959	42,037	13,547	28,490	329,268
1960	49,600	15,972	33,628	357,758
1961	44,862	16,040	28,822	391,386
1962	42,696	15,847	26,849	420,208
1963	40,893	18,521	22,372	447,057
1964	49,035	18,532	30,503	469,429
1965	54,474	20,062	34,412	499,932
1966	58,400	20,048	38,352	534,344
1967				572,696

Source: Jamaica Department of Statistics, National Income and Product, 1967, Accounts I and V (Kingston, April,
1968).

salaries and direct welfare payments, but these are in the
nature of consumption and are treated in the same way as all
other government consumption expenditures.)

The public sector outlay for welfare investment can be obtained by examining the actual and planned expenditures of the
Jamaican government's capital account, as shown in Table 21.

Welfare investment, represented by categories 2 and 3,
includes expenditures of fixed capital for health, sanitation,
education, and public housing. Total welfare investment can
be expressed as follows:

Welfare Investment = Ownership of Private Dwellings
+ .4755 (Government Investment)
1957-62
+ .5120 (Government Investment)
1963-68.

TABLE 20

Calculation of Rate of Capital Consumption
Allowance, Jamaica, 1959-66
(1960 Constant Prices--In Thousands
of Jamaican Pounds)

Year	Capital Consumption Allowance	Total Capital Stock (K')	Rate of Capital Consumption Allowance (d)
1959	13,547	329,268	.04114
1960	15,972	357,758	.04464
1961	16,040	391,386	.04098
1962	15,847	420,208	.03771
1963	18,521	447,057	.04143
1964	18,532	469,429	.03948
1965	20,062	499,932	.04013
1966	20,048	534,344	.03752
			$d = .04038$
			$= .04$

TABLE 21

Actual and Planned Expenditures of Government
Capital Account, Jamaica, 1957-68
(In Millions of Jamaican Pounds)

Services	Actual Expenditure 1957-62	Planned Expenditure 1963-68
Economic Services	19.5	38.6
Social Services	8.7	21.1
Community Services	11.7	25.7
General	3.0	6.0
Total	42.9	91.4

Source: Jamaica Ministry of Development and Welfare, Five Year Independence Plan 1963-1968 (Kingston, 1963), p. 52.

It can be seen that planned public welfare investment approximates 51.2 percent of total government investment. Government investment, in turn, has averaged 19.4 percent of all investment. Calculations for total welfare investment, including the private sector, are shown in Table 22.

For the 1959-66 period, 19.96 percent of gross domestic investment was for welfare purposes. Conversely, 80.04 percent of gross investment was for fixed productive stock. On the assumption that approximately four-fifths of existing total capital stock is productive in nature, the estimate of productive capital stock, K, in Jamaica for 1967 is:

$$£J572,696,000 \times .8004 = £J458,386,000.$$

Welfare investment, hitherto, has been discussed only in terms of its having to be netted out to determine productive fixed capital formation and productive capital stock. The concept used in determining its own value is that welfare investment is increased in the same proportion from year to year as increases for all other government expenditures, plus an allowance for welfare investment outlays, at current per capita levels, for net increases in the population. The first step, therefore, is determination of the marginal propensity of government consumption, h, as is shown in Table 23.

Government consumption in a given year is equal to the level of expenditure for the previous year plus the marginal propensity to consume out of the increase in gross national product. The value of this marginal propensity of government consumption, h, approximates .1850 in Jamaica and is somewhat greater than the average propensity in developed countries. In most developing countries, government consumption has been growing, relative to private consumption, with indications from a study covering more than forty such countries of marginal propensities of government consumption approaching .20.[3]

Once aggregate government consumption has been determined, the per capital values (measured in terms of equivalent adult consumers) can be readily calculated. This ratio of per capita government consumption from one year to the next (gc_t/gc_{t-1}) is used to determine the level of welfare investment for the existing population--consumption deepening. This amount of welfare investment, when calculated on a per capita basis, is then used to determine welfare investment for net additions to the population--consumption widening.

Estimates of productive capital stock for years beyond 1970 include allowance for demographic investment. Along with welfare investment, demographic investment is subtracted

TABLE 22

Welfare Investment, Jamaica, 1959-66
(1960 Constant Prices--In Thousands of Jamaican Pounds)

Year	Gross Domestic Investment (I)	Government Investment	Government Welfare Investment	+ Private Housing Investment	= Welfare Investment (WI)	WI/I (Percent)
1959	47,561	5,365	2,500	6,837	9,387	19.74
1960	51,888	5,294	2,517	8,544	11,061	21.32
1961	48,195	4,977	2,374	6,731	9,105	18.89
1962	45,187	4,331	2,060	5,992	8,052	17.84
1963	44,304	4,548	2,328	5,467	7,795	17.59
1964	52,326	6,061	3,103	7,547	10,650	20.35
1965	56,307	8,377	4,289	8,542	12,831	22.79
1966	60,923	9,338	4,781	8,131	12,912	21.19

Average WI/I--19.96 Percent

Source: Jamaica Department of Statistics, National Income and Production, 1967, (Kingston, April, 1968), Table I, "Fixed Capital Formation by Industrial Sectors."

TABLE 23

Calculation of Marginal Propensity of Government Consumption, Jamaica

(In Thousands of Jamaican Pounds)

Year	Government Consumption[a] (GC)	Price Deflator	Inverse	Government Consumption[b] (GC)	ΔGC	Gross National Product[b] (Y)	ΔY	Marginal Propensity of Government Consumption (GC/ΔY) h
1959	19,568	99.8	100.20	19,607	-	215,096	-	-
1960	21,610	100.0	100.00	21,610	2,003	227,258	12,162	.1647
1961	24,179	105.1	95.15	23,006	1,396	232,387	5,219	.2722
1962	27,167	108.1	92.51	25,132	2,126	237,492	5,105	.4165
1963	29,309	110.1	90.83	26,621	1,489	245,661	8,169	.1823
1964	31,803	115.1	86.88	27,630	1,009	267,890	22,229	.0455
1965	34,919	117.9	84.82	29,618	1,988	286,037	18,147	.1095
1966	37,111	122.1	81.90	30,394	776	293,483	7,446	.1042

Marginal Propensity of Government Consumption, h = .1850

a Current prices.
b 1960 constant prices.

74

from <u>total</u> net fixed capital formation, J', in order to determine net fixed <u>productive</u> capital formation, J.

In Jamaica, at present, there is no real indication of the
cost per acceptor of birth control. Such cost includes rent for
buildings, salaries and wages of staff, and cost of contraceptive supplies prorated on a yearly basis for the equivalent
number of acceptors. Lacking the kind of records from which
costs can be assigned or continuation rates determined, one
can only hazard a guess as to what the costs per acceptor might
be.

As a reasonable guess, the average cost per birth control
acceptor is figured at £J2. If, in the future, the program ex-
pands, proportionately more acceptors may be recruited
through out-reach programs, which will tend to raise the cost
per acceptor. This rise can be balanced, however, by fuller
utilization of clinics and personnel, which will tend to lower
the cost per acceptor. The sum of £J2 ($4.80) is more than
double the amount of $2, suggested by Enke as representative
of a developing country and which may be regarded as reasonably conservative. [4] In actual practice, the sums needed
to bring about stipulated fertility reductions are quite minor.
Doubling or even quadrupling the cost per acceptor will have
little effect on the amount of fixed productive capital formation.

SAVINGS

As already indicated, the savings rate used in the model
differs from most others in that it represents the average
propensity to save before allowance for increases in government and private consumption for net additions to the population. The concept implies that the need to make provision for
consumption-widening expenditures due to net population
growth reduces the amount that is actually saved. The average
propensity to save is regarded as constant from year to year.
The amount of domestic savings, however, varies with the
consumption demands made by net additions to the population.

For this study, savings were calculated by expressing
government consumption and private consumption in constant
prices for the period 1959-66 by means of separate component
price deflators to get total consumption figures for each of the
years. Differences in population, ΔP, were obtained from
successive estimates of mean population. Total consumption
per capita, tc, was then derived by dividing total consumption

by the mean population of each year.   This per capita figure,
when multiplied by the net change in population (tc ΔP), gives
the consumption-widening component for the periods, as shown
in Table 24.

The increase in consumption due to net additions to the
population in Jamaica approximates 2 percent.   This means
that both the average and marginal propensities to save for
Jamaica are actually .02 higher than if provision were not
needed for net additions to the population.

The next step is postulating a reasonable value or series
of values for e, the savings rate obtaining without allowance
for increases in consumption for net additions in population.
The savings function in the model is based on the average
propensity to save--the proportion of domestic saving to gross
national product--rather than on the marginal propensity to
save--the increase in saving as a proportion of increase in
gross national product.   Either concept could have been employed in the model; average propensity is chosen for ease of
calculation and stability.   Calculations for both are shown in
Table 25.

As indicated, recent values of both the average and marginal propensities to save for Jamaica closely approximate
.18.   In another study, values for the marginal gross saving
ratio in Jamaica were estimated at .16 (historical), .18 (current and planned), and .20 (upper limit). [5] If, as was initially
done in this model, high, medium, and low values of the savings coefficient are postulated, the framework limits cited
can serve as a guideline.

The value of the savings coefficient, e, is higher by .02
than that observed, because it represents savings before allowance for increased consumption due to net additions in
population.   Reasonable corresponding values of the savings
coefficient are .18, .20, and .22.

Actual calculation of f, the coefficient representing the
proportion of net borrowing from abroad to the arithmetic
mean of the gross national product for the previous five years
is as follows:

$$f = \frac{E_{1962} + E_{1963} + E_{1964} + E_{1965} + E_{1966}}{Y_{1957} + Y_{1958} + Y_{1959} + Y_{1960} + Y_{1961}} = .0370$$

In similar manner, g, the coefficient representing the
proportion of net foreign transfer payments to the arithmetic
mean of the previous five years gross national product was
found to be .0229.   Both of these coefficients are used as con-
stants in the model.

TABLE 24

Calculation of Consumption "Widening" To Make Provision for
Net Additions to Population, Jamaica, 1960-66
(In Thousands of Jamaican Pounds)

Year	Mean Population (P)	ΔP	Government Consumption (GC)	Private Consumption (PC)	Total Consumption (TC)	Per Capita Total Consumption (tc)	Provision for Net Additions to Population (tc ΔP)
1959	1,598.4	-	19,607	164,799	184,306	115.30	-
1960	1,628.2	29.8	21,610	169,237	190,847	117.21	3,493
1961	1,646.2	18.0	23,006	171,688	194,694	118.27	2,129
1962	1,659.8	13.6	25,132	182,460	207,592	125.07	1,701
1963	1,696.5	36.7	26,621	185,418	212,039	124.99	3,587
1964	1,739.8	43.3	27,630	208,270	235,900	135.59	5,871
1965	1,788.2	48.4	29,618	215,405	245,023	137.02	6,632
1966	1,836.7	48.5	30,394	222,353	252,747	137.61	6,674

$$\frac{tc\ \Delta P}{TC} = .0196 \quad \text{or } 1.96 \text{ percent}$$

TABLE 25

Calculation of Marginal and Average Propensities To Save, Jamaica, 1959-66
(1960 Constant Prices--In Thousands of Jamaican Pounds)

Year	Gross Domestic Saving (B)	Gross National Product (Y)	B/Y	Marginal Propensity to Save
1959	37,761	215,096	.1756	
1960	42,396	227,258	.1866	$a = \dfrac{B_n - B_o}{Y_n - Y_o}$
1961	45,699	232,387	.1967	
1962	44,192	237,492	.1861	$= \dfrac{51,526 - 37,761}{293,483 - 215,096}$
1963	47,877	245,661	.1949	
1964	41,280	267,890	.1541	$= .1756$
1965	48,668	286,037	.1701	
1966	51,526	293,483	.1756	

Average Propensity to Save = .1800

NOTES

1.   Jamaica Department of Statistics, Industrial Activity, Mining, Manufacture, Construction, 1960 (Kingston, 1963).

2.   Jamaica Department of Statistics, National Income and Product, 1967 (Kingston, 1968), Table I, "Gross Fixed Capital Formation."

3.   Hollis B. Chenery and Alan M. Strout, "Foreign Assistance and Economic Development," The American Economic Review, LVI, 4 (September, 1966), 712.

4.   Stephen Enke and Richard G. Zind, "Effect of Fewer Births on Average Income," Journal of Biosocial Sciences, I, 1 (1969), 45.   Originally published by Enke as Raising Per Capita Income Through Fewer Births (Santa Barbara, Calif.: TEMPO, General Electric Center for Advanced Studies, 1967).

5.   Chenery and Strout, op. cit., p. 712.

CHAPTER **5** RESULTS OF THE
SIMULATIONS

DEMOGRAPHIC FINDINGS

There is absolutely no question that there will be marked
growth in Jamaica's population during the next fifty years.
The only question is how great this increase is likely to be.

If present high-fertility rates continue, population in
this island of 4,550 square miles will increase from approximately 2 million persons in 1970 to nearly 14 million by 2020.
The medium fertility assumption, which postulates a decline
by 2020 to one-half of present fertility rates (1 percent a year
reduction), will generate a population of close to 9 million.
Even a low assumption of a decline to one-half present fertility
rates by 1995 (2 percent a year reduction) will still produce
a population of 7 million by 2020. The extreme assumption
that a zero growth rate will prevail between 1995 and 2020
(3 percent a year reduction) can occur only after the population already totals more than 4 million persons. Fifty years
hence, population will have increased under the four fertility
assumptions by 700, 450, 350, and 200 percent, respectively,
as is shown in Table 26.

Age Structure and Dependency Ratios

Of equal importance to numbers are the differences in
age-groupings under the various fertility assumptions. The
effects on composition of population are greatest between
high and very low fertility assumptions. The zero to fourteen
age group under high, constant fertility remains at about 47
percent of total population over time, with those sixty-five
and over being only 3 percent, and persons in the productive
ages, fifteen to sixty-four, approximating 50 percent. The
results obtaining under very low fertility assumptions show
the zero to fourteen age group stabilizing at about 13 percent

80

TABLE 26

Demographic Projections, Under
Various Fertility Assumptions, Jamaica, 1970-2020
(In Millions)

Year	High	Medium	Low	Very Low
1970	2.093	2.093	2.093	2.093
1980	2.995	2.942	2.888	2.834
1990	4.361	4.069	3.794	3.512
2000	6.394	5.503	4.719	3.849
2010	9.992	7.190	5.818	4.055
2020	13.936	8.985	7.004	4.136

by 2020, with those sixty-five and over comprising 10 percent. The productive age group of fifteen to sixty-four by this time becomes 77 percent of the total population.

Values for medium and low fertility assumptions fall somewhere in between those cited. As contrasted with high fertility, the zero to fourteen age groups are a progressively smaller proportion of total population and fifteen to sixty-four progressively larger, with sixty-five and over showing a small but positive increase. These differentials are tied very closely to the reproductive levels of the past, and the greatest proportionate changes, as indicated in the projections, occur in the last fifteen years of this century and the first five years of the twenty-first century, as shown in Table 27.

Dependency ratios, defined here as the quotient of those in the productive ages from fifteen to sixty-four divided by those in the dependent ages of zero to fourteen and sixty-five and over, also show large differentials over time. The high fertility projection gives a dependency ratio around 100 throughout the fifty-year period. Under medium fertility, the dependency ratio falls steadily to a value of sixty-two by 2020. The low assumption flattens out to fifty-six by the year 2005 and remains at that level. The dependency ratio under very low fertility declines very rapidly to a level of twenty-six by 2010, but with an increasing proportion of persons

TABLE 27

Percent Distribution of Population, by Broad Age Groups, Under
Various Fertility Assumptions, Jamaica, 1970-2020

Year	Zero to Fourteen				Fifteen to Sixty-four				Sixty-five and Over			
	High	Medium	Low	Very Low	High	Medium	Low	Very Low	High	Medium	Low	Very Low
1970	45.7	45.7	45.7	45.7	50.1	50.1	50.1	50.1	4.2	4.2	4.2	4.2
1980	46.0	45.0	44.0	42.9	49.6	50.5	51.5	52.4	4.4	4.5	4.5	4.6
1990	47.3	43.8	40.0	35.5	49.1	52.3	55.8	60.0	3.6	3.9	4.1	4.5
2000	47.0	41.1	34.1	22.8	50.2	55.7	62.2	72.7	2.8	3.2	3.7	4.6
2010	47.1	37.8	31.7	14.2	50.3	58.8	64.1	79.6	2.6	3.4	4.2	6.1
2020	47.0	33.8	30.3	13.1	50.1	61.7	63.9	77.1	2.9	4.5	5.8	9.8

sixty-five and over, rises to thirty by 2020. Whereas, under
high fertility, the number of persons in the productive ages
is just about equal to the number of children and older people,
this ratio almost doubles under the medium and low fertility
assumptions and triples under conditions of very low fertility,
as shown in Table 28.

TABLE 28

Dependency Ratios, Under Varying Fertility
Assumptions, Jamaica, 1970-2020

Year	High	Medium	Low	Very Low
1970	99.8	99.8	99.8	99.8
1980	101.5	97.9	94.3	90.7
1990	103.7	91.0	79.1	66.6
2000	99.1	79.5	60.8	37.6
2010	98.7	70.0	56.0	25.6
2020	99.7	62.2	56.6	29.6

Labor Force and Equivalent Adult Consumers

There is a need, also, to examine the annual growth rate
of labor force as compared to equivalent adult consumers.
To the extent that labor force grows more rapidly than the body
of nonproductive members of the population, a country can
raise significantly total and per capita output. If, however,
equivalent consumers are growing more rapidly than the labor
to fulfill consumption demands, more of the national product
will be diverted to meet consumption needs, and living standards will fail to rise as rapidly as they could have under conditions in which the labor ratio was favorable.

The differences in growth rates between labor force and
equivalent adult consumers are set forth in Table 29. For the
period 1970-80, differences among fertility assumptions are

due only to the effects of reduced births on equivalent adult
consumers. After 1985, these differences become more pronounced because of the effects of reduced births on the number
of persons entering the labor force. Under low fertility,
labor-force growth is particularly favorable through 2020,
with the advantage over high fertility reaching a peak in 1995.
By 2010, the transition from a very young population to one
of mature age composition has been completed, and consumption needs begin to grow more rapidly than labor force. By
this time, however, the degree of economic growth made
possible under low fertility is so markedly greater than under
high fertility that differences between labor and consumption
growth rates are of lessened importance.

TABLE 29

Difference Between Annual Growth Rates of Labor
Force and Equivalent Adult Consumers, Under Various
Fertility Assumptions, Jamaica, 1970-2020

Year	High	Medium	Low	Very Low
1970	.14	.16	.18	0.20
1980	-.21	.01	.18	0.37
1990	.13	.43	.75	1.11
2000	.15	.39	.58	1.09
2010	.05	.27	-.07	0.11
2020	.06	.20	-.11	-0.46

Births Prevented and Acceptors Needed

All of the differences in the demographic results displayed
in the model are the results of births that have been prevented
by securing the number of acceptors needed to bring about
stipulated reductions in fertility. In the model, both births

and deaths are calculated by five-year time periods. The
number of acceptors and births prevented must necessarily
be estimated in the same way. Because population is measured
in terms of a given year, acceptors and births prevented must
be expressed as an average yearly number. (The high fertility
assumption involving neither births prevented nor requisite
numbers of acceptors is not considered.)

Some interesting patterns emerge among the three levels
of fertility reduction. The medium pattern has the least number of acceptors and births prevented for about forty years.
After this time, the population of women at risk is so large
that the smaller proportion of acceptors needed under the
medium fertility assumption exceeds the larger proportion of
acceptors needed under the low fertility assumption. Thus,
acceptors needed and births prevented under medium fertility
exceed those under low after 2010 and very low after 2015.

Even the modest goal of medium reduction of fertility
rates to one-half present levels in fifty years may require
increasingly substantial inputs throughout the period. The
last five-year period, 2015-20, would necessitate having
1,038,600 women per year as acceptors, or 27 percent more
than the average of 817,400 women per year in the previous
five-year period. (Contrast this number with the minimal
average number of 12,400 for the 1970-75 period.) For every
person availing herself of family planning services in the
initial period, eighty-six persons will need to receive services
fifty years hence if a 1 percent reduction in fertility rates is
to be continued.

The number of acceptors needed under low fertility reduction has its greatest proportionate growth up through 2000,
and while continuing to rise throughout the fifty-year period,
shows signs of leveling off at perhaps 1 million women by 2030.
The low assumption, having reached the goal of halving fertility rates in twenty-five years rather then the fifty years of
the medium assumption, does not make comparable gains in
the number of births prevented after 1995. Births prevented,
in the period 1995-2020, increase by 430 percent under condition of medium fertility reduction but by only 72 percent
under the low reduction.

The pattern of acceptors under the very low assumption
differs from the other two in rising rapidly in the earlier
years, reaching a peak of 1,065,000 acceptors between 2005
and 2010 and declining to under 1 million acceptors by 2020.
The sharper, earlier decline in fertility (hence, a reduced
population growth) gives the greatest advantage to the very low

assumption in second-round effects. This advantage is offset, somewhat, by the upward shift in age composition for those at risk, as compared to patterns obtaining under lower rates of fertility reduction. To prevent a given number of births, the fewest number of acceptors is needed under medium fertility, a slightly higher number under low, and still greater number under very low, as is shown in Table 30.

The number of births occurring (or prevented) is a function both of fertility rates and the number of women of childbearing age. All three fertility reduction projections are affected by past patterns of fertility. The present high level of births in Jamaica means that a large number of potential mothers must be taken into account for a number of years in the future. The number of women entering into childbearing ages can only be reduced after a period of fifteen years or more, when fertility reduction programs have had time to operate.

The population of 14 million in 2020, given no reduction in fertility, is 55 percent greater than the population of 9 million obtaining under the medium level of fertility reduction. The proportion of women in childbearing ages is somewhat more favorable in the medium situation, but even the effect of lowering fertility rates to half the present level may be far from sufficient for the country. The goals of fertility reduction should be set still higher and reduction must be effected more quickly. Given the handicap of the past legacy of births, policy planners find that the effect of a fertility reduction program is offset by the constantly increasing numbers of women in the childbearing ages.

The low assumption, which reaches the same level of fertility reduction as medium in half the time, is still more favorably constituted in that its total population is 2 million less than medium in 2020 and in that it has a population with a more favorable age composition. Absolute growth in population size occurs in the twenty-five years following 1995, however, even though the goal of reducing fertility rates to half the present levels is reached. This unfortunate truth reinforces the conclusion that whereas an earlier effort in fertility reduction has more impact than the equivalent effort at a later date, cutting fertility rates by half is not in itself sufficient to bring population growth under control. The 2 percent reduction of fertility rates per year as postulated in the low assumption should be carried well past the first twenty-five years. It may not be possible to maintain a 2 percent rate of reduction for too many years after 1995 (this would imply

TABLE 30

Average Yearly Number of Acceptors and Births Prevented,
Under Various Fertility Assumptions, Jamaica, 1970-2020

Years	Medium		Low		Very Low	
	Acceptors	Births Prevented	Acceptors	Births Prevented	Acceptors	Births Prevented
1970-75	12,400	2,400	24,800	5,000	37,000	7,200
1975-80	44,800	8,800	90,000	17,800	134,800	26,600
1980-85	100,400	19,400	179,800	35,600	269,800	53,400
1985-90	151,600	29,600	302,000	59,000	451,600	88,200
1990-95	234,000	45,200	460,600	88,800	680,200	131,200
1995-2000	349,600	65,000	596,000	113,400	943,800	179,000
2000-2005	471,800	89,800	675,600	127,000	1,027,200	190,400
2005-10	629,400	119,800	743,600	138,000	1,065,000	191,200
2010-15	817,400	148,800	804,000	145,800	1,044,600	177,800
2015-20	1,038,600	194,600	865,800	152,800	985,600	153,600

no births at all in fifty years), but continuation of further
fertility reduction should be attempted for at least a few years
after this time.

The very low fertility projection represents a maximum
degree of fertility reduction, and there is some question as
to whether the goal of 3 percent reduction per year is entirely
feasible. The legacy of large numbers of people, not in the
childbearing ages, who continue to live during the period of
rapid fertility reduction, must be taken into account. If the
zero growth rate is not approached gradually, there may be
too few people in the reproductive ages to maintain existing
levels of population, with a later consequent need for a policy
of encouraging the raising of fertility rates. (The problem of
transition from high to low fertility rates is, of course, made
much easier if the level of the initial rates is lower.) This
difficulty has been obviated in the model by easing off the
3 percent reduction rate and allowing the "braking distance"
in obtaining a zero growth rate to be expanded over a twenty-
five year period. Projected population growth, while very
low, still approximates .4 percent a year from 1995 to 2020.
Age-sex composition is being normalized during this period
and future prospects of population stability increasingly
assured.

ECONOMIC FINDINGS

The economic part of the model uses such demographic
outputs as equivalent adult consumers and working-age population. Demographic outputs are also used to compute demographic investment and welfare investment. The three values
of average savings propensities (.22, .20, .18) were substituted
under varying fertility assumptions in experimentations with
the model, with the result that the higher the savings coefficient,
the higher the capital-labor ratio and the lower the marginal
productivity of capital. Similarly, estimates of gross national
product with an average propensity to save of .22 are higher
than estimates of gross national product with a saving rate of
.18. Estimates of gross national product under high and low
propensities to save range from a difference of 15 percent
under low productivity (.3), to 30 percent under medium capital productivity (.5), and to 50 percent under high productivity
(.7). These observed differences are also very nearly the
same for all fertility assumptions.

As stated earlier, the propensity to save, as used in this
model, is defined as the propensity to save prior to making
allowance for private and public consumption needs for net
additions to the population. Whereas the total amount of
savings is affected by differences in the rate of growth of
population, as reflected by the four fertility assumptions,
the basic propensity to save is not. Variations in the amount
of saving, therefore, are induced only by changes in the net
additions to the population. To simplify, a single propensity
to save of .20 was adopted because it most nearly approximates the observed marginal and average propensities to save.
There are sufficient other variations of capital and labor productivities so that projections based on variations in the savings
coefficient would tend only to obscure the other demographic-
econometric relationships.

Gross National Product

A second simplification was to include the effects of returns to scale only when no autonomous growth is postulated.
As implied in the definition, output under any given assumption
of fertility and productivity of capital is greatest under increasing returns to scale, somewhat lower under constant
returns, and lowest under decreasing returns to scale. Output increases through time, with a sixfold increase in fifty
years registered for high fertility and low productivity of
capital and a thirty-sevenfold gain for very low fertility and
very high productivity of capital.

The differentials among returns to scale are primarily
a function of time and productivity of capital. Under low
productivity of capital, the year 2020 shows a difference in
product somewhat less than double, i.e., between increasing
and decreasing returns to scale. (This proportion declines
slightly from high to very low fertility.) Under medium productivity of capital, differences in product, generally, are at
least double, and under high capital productivity, returns to
scale reflect a tripling of differences in product, as shown in
Table 31.

These differences in product between increasing and
decreasing returns to scale are of the same magnitude, even
when product is measured per equivalent adult consumer.
Whereas projected total gross national product for 2020 tends
to decrease when one moves from high to low fertility assumptions (more marked under low than high capital productivity),

TABLE 31

Gross National Product, No Autonomous Growth, Under
Various Fertility Assumptions, Jamaica, 1970-2020
(In Millions of Jamaican Pounds--Savings Coefficient =. 20)

Low Productivity of Capital (.3)

(a)

Decreasing Returns to Scale

Year	High	Medium	Low	Very Low
1970	334.1	334.1	334.1	334.1
1980	467.9	468.3	468.7	469.2
1990	642.5	643.8	644.9	646.2
2000	893.2	878.9	865.9	851.8
2010	1225.1	1163.6	1092.6	1020.5
2020	1661.3	1483.2	1307.9	1081.2

(b)

Constant Returns to Scale

Year	High	Medium	Low	Very Low
1970	338.8	338.8	338.8	338.8
1980	495.5	496.0	496.5	496.9
1990	716.7	717.7	718.5	719.5
2000	1061.5	1038.1	1016.8	994.1
2010	1559.8	1455.2	1342.1	1228.9
2020	2279.7	1956.4	1669.2	1316.5

(c)

Increasing Returns to Scale

Year	High	Medium	Low	Very Low
1970	343.7	343.7	343.7	343.7
1980	524.9	525.3	525.8	526.3
1990	799.4	800.1	800.5	801.2
2000	1259.6	1224.4	1192.7	1159.0
2010	1974.7	1811.7	1642.5	1475.6
2020	3083.6	2555.3	2114.6	1594.9

Medium Productivity of Capital (.5)

(a)
Decreasing Returns to Scale

Year	High	Medium	Low	Very Low
1970	335.7	335.7	335.7	335.7
1980	480.5	481.3	482.1	482.9
1990	660.7	665.5	670.2	675.2
2000	897.3	902.8	908.4	914.4
2010	1185.9	1187.8	1170.9	1157.0
2020	1520.2	1510.8	1438.5	1327.3

(b)
Constant Returns to Scale

Year	High	Medium	Low	Very Low
1970	340.7	340.7	340.7	340.7
1980	512.7	513.5	514.4	515.2
1990	753.7	758.8	763.6	768.8
2000	1118.0	1116.5	1115.5	1114.7
2010	1643.9	1604.8	1544.1	1486.9
2020	2401.1	2234.4	2024.9	1754.1

(c)
Increasing Returns to Scale

Year	High	Medium	Low	Very Low
1970	345.7	345.7	345.7	345.7
1980	547.1	548.0	548.9	549.8
1990	859.8	865.1	870.1	875.5
2000	1388.6	1376.7	1366.4	1355.7
2010	2246.1	2144.2	2018.4	1898.0
2020	3633.8	3216.6	2796.0	2289.1

continued

TABLE 31 - continued

High Productivity of Capital (.7)

(a)
Decreasing Returns to Scale

Year	High	Medium	Low	Very Low
1970	337.3	337.3	337.3	337.3
1980	496.8	479.9	499.2	500.4
1990	693.2	702.8	712.1	722.0
2000	930.2	962.0	993.6	1028.9
2010	1186.6	1276.2	1342.1	1426.4
2020	1413.5	1644.6	1753.1	1873.1

(b)
Constant Returns to Scale

Year	High	Medium	Low	Very Low
1970	342.4	342.4	342.4	342.4
1980	534.7	535.9	537.3	538.6
1990	814.7	825.5	835.9	847.0
2000	1239.8	1270.5	1301.1	1335.8
2010	1870.6	1938.9	1972.5	2027.2
2020	2803.5	2917.7	2882.0	2741.4

(c)
Increasing Returns to Scale

Year	High	Medium	Low	Very Low
1970	347.6	347.6	347.6	347.6
1980	575.6	577.1	578.5	580.0
1990	957.8	969.9	981.6	994.1
2000	1643.9	1670.5	1697.3	1728.4
2010	2865.8	2883.6	2851.9	2845.8
2020	5048.9	4892.4	4560.9	4159.0

Very High Productivity of Capital (1.0), with Constant Returns to Scale

Year	High	Medium	Low	Very Low
1970	344.7	344.7	344.7	344.7
1980	580.1	582.3	584.6	586.9
1990	995.8	1021.6	1047.2	1074.7
2000	1767.0	1909.7	2059.3	2238.4
2010	3277.0	3873.8	4467.0	5332.7
2020	6380.3	8561.1	10473.9	12633.0

the projected per capita gross national product increases
markedly as fertility rates decline. For example, gross
national product, with constant returns to scale and a low
productivity of capital, is projected at £J2,280 million under
high fertility. The corresponding estimate under low fertility
is £J1,317 million, or about 42 percent less. However, when
product is measured on a per capita basis, product increases
from £J213 to £J338, as between high and low fertility, an
increase of 59 percent.

The importance of the analysis of returns to scale is that,
when output is measured on a per capita basis, a lower level
of fertility can more than offset less favorable returns to
scale. For example, regardless of the productivity of capital,
per capita output is higher under the low fertility assumption,
even under decreasing returns to scale, than is the corresponding output under high fertility and constant returns to
scale. Or, using the extreme case, output per head fifty
years hence is higher under very low fertility and decreasing
returns to scale than the corresponding figure under high
fertility and increasing returns to scale, as shown in Table 32.

For reasons cited previously, the most likely trend in
developing countries is for decreasing returns to scale. However, to be guardedly optimistic (and to facilitate comparison
with other studies that have not considered the effects of
scale), further analysis, here, will assume constant returns
to scale only.

A third simplification is that, with the exception of describing gross national product with and without autonomous
growth, discussion of findings of the economic model will be
limited to results obtaining under a low productivity of capital.
This assumption produces the most conservative estimates of
economic growth and maximizes the contribution to production
by labor, while, at the same time, minimizing the contribution
by capital. Differences in total and per capita economic indices can thus be ascribed to the various fertility assumptions
used. Table 33 shows for constant returns to scale and low
productivity of labor, the gross national product per equivalent adult consumer under various fertility assumptions in
terms of base year 1967=100. Increases in output per head
are, respectively, 4.7, 27.5, 37.0, and 66.5 percent higher
in 2020 under the successive assumptions of fertility reduction.

TABLE 32

Gross National Product Per Equivalent Adult Consumer,
No Autonomous Growth, Under Various Fertility Assumptions,
Jamaica, 1970-2020
(In Millions of Jamaican Pounds--Savings Coefficient =.20)

Low Productivity of Capital (.3)

(a)
Decreasing Returns to Scale

Year	High	Medium	Low	Very Low
1970	204.9	204.9	204.9	204.9
1980	202.4	204.4	206.4	208.5
1990	192.0	200.8	209.8	219.9
2000	181.8	199.1	218.4	244.8
2010	168.9	197.4	221.5	269.8
2020	155.1	196.4	218.1	277.8

(b)
Constant Returns to Scale

Year	High	Medium	Low	Very Low
1970	207.8	207.8	207.8	207.8
1980	214.4	216.5	218.6	220.8
1990	214.2	223.8	233.7	244.8
2000	216.0	235.1	256.5	285.7
2010	215.1	246.9	272.0	324.9
2020	212.9	259.1	278.3	338.3

(c)
Increasing Returns to Scale

Year	High	Medium	Low	Very Low
1970	210.8	210.8	210.8	210.8
1980	227.1	229.3	231.6	233.9
1990	238.9	249.5	260.4	272.6
2000	256.3	277.4	300.9	333.1
2010	272.3	307.4	332.9	390.2
2020	287.9	338.4	352.6	409.8

Medium Productivity of Capital (.5)

(a)
Decreasing Returns to Scale

Year	High	Medium	Low	Very Low
1970	205.9	205.9	205.9	205.9
1980	207.9	210.1	212.3	214.6
1990	197.4	207.6	218.0	229.7
2000	182.6	204.5	229.2	262.8
2010	163.5	201.5	237.3	305.9
2020	141.9	200.1	239.9	341.1

(b)
Constant Returns to Scale

Year	High	Medium	Low	Very Low
1970	208.9	208.9	208.9	208.9
1980	224.1	221.8	226.5	229.0
1990	236.6	225.2	248.4	261.6
2000	252.9	227.5	281.4	320.3
2010	272.3	226.7	313.0	393.2
2020	295.9	224.2	337.6	450.7

(c)
Increasing Returns to Scale

Year	High	Medium	Low	Very Low
1970	212.0	212.0	212.0	212.0
1980	236.7	239.2	241.8	244.4
1990	256.9	269.8	283.0	297.9
2000	282.6	311.9	344.7	389.6
2010	309.7	363.8	409.1	501.9
2020	339.3	426.0	466.2	588.2

continued

TABLE 32 - continued

High Productivity of Capital (.7)

(a)
Decreasing Returns to Scale

Year	High	Medium	Low	Very Low
1970	206.8	206.8	206.8	206.8
1980	214.9	217.3	219.8	222.4
1990	207.1	219.2	231.6	245.7
2000	189.3	217.9	250.7	295.7
2010	163.6	216.5	272.0	377.2
2020	132.0	217.8	292.3	481.3

(b)
Constant Returns to Scale

Year	High	Medium	Low	Very Low
1970	210.0	210.0	210.0	210.0
1980	231.3	233.9	236.6	239.4
1990	243.4	257.4	271.9	288.2
2000	252.3	287.8	328.2	383.9
2010	258.0	328.9	399.8	536.0
2020	261.8	386.4	480.6	725.9

(c)
Increasing Returns to Scale

Year	High	Medium	Low	Very Low
1970	213.2	213.2	213.2	213.2
1980	249.0	251.9	254.8	257.8
1990	286.2	302.5	319.3	338.3
2000	334.5	378.4	428.2	496.7
2010	395.2	489.2	578.1	752.5
2020	471.4	648.0	760.5	1068.7

Very High Productivity of Capital (1.0), with Constant Returns to Scale

Year	High	Medium	Low	Very Low
1970	211.4	211.4	211.4	211.4
1980	250.9	254.2	257.5	260.8
1990	297.5	318.6	340.6	365.7
2000	359.6	432.6	519.5	643.3
2010	451.9	657.2	905.5	1410.0
2020	595.7	1133.9	1746.5	3583.7

TABLE 33

Gross National Product Per Equivalent Adult
Consumer[a] Expressed in Terms of Base 1967=100,
Under Various Fertility Assumptions, Jamaica, 1970-2020
(Low Productivity of Capital, .3--Constant Returns to Scale)

Year	High	Medium	Low	Very Low
1970	102.2	102.2	102.2	102.2
1980	105.5	106.5	107.5	108.6
1990	105.4	110.8	115.0	120.4
2000	106.2	115.6	126.2	140.5
2010	105.8	121.4	133.8	159.8
2020	104.7	127.4	136.9	166.4

[a]Expressed in terms of base 1967=100.

The results of including an allowance for autonomous
growth of 1.5 percent a year are reflected in Table 34. Under
low capital productivity, gross national product in 2020 with
provision for autonomous growth is about 2.6 percent higher
than would be obtained without autonomous growth. When
capital productivity is very high, however, these differentials
in 2020 average 26.6 percent higher with antonomous growth.
What this increase demonstrates is that the level of capital
productivity is a key to future growth. The added product
from autonomous growth tends to be far less when capital
productivity is low than when the productivity of capital is
high. Because the impact of technological change will be less
than otherwise if the contribution of capital to output is low,
a case could be built for advocating increased capital-intensive
investment in developing countries as a means of encouraging
autonomous growth.

Changes in Employment

A major variant concerning the contribution of labor to
output was also tried out. The available labor force was

TABLE 34

Average Relative Differences in Gross National Product
With and Without Autonomous Growth,[a]
Under All Fertility Assumptions, Jamaica, 1970-2020[b]
(Constant Returns to Scale--Savings Coefficient =.20)
1967=100

Year	Low Productivity of Capital (.3)	Very High Productivity of Capital (1.0)
1970	101.7	102.1
1980	102.0	104.4
1990	102.3	107.8
2000	102.4	111.8
2010	102.5	120.5
2020	102.6	126.6

[a]Autonomous growth of 1.5 percent per year.
[b]Base 1967=100.

calculated by use of age-sex specific participation rates
rather than by use of the whole of the population between fifteen
and sixty-four. Starting with an initial unemployment rate of
13 percent in 1967, subsequent estimates of employed labor
were derived through a mechanism that increased or decreased
rates of unemployment depending on the extent to which the
growth rate of productive capital exceeded the growth rate of
available labor.

Far less additional employment is generated under conditions of low capital productivity than under high capital
productivity. Unemployment initially declines under conditions
of low capital productivity, then rises to levels in excess of
base-year values, followed by a decline to the end of the fifty-
year period. The higher the level of fertility, the later the
period of peak unemployment and the greater the amount of
unemployment. Under high fertility, unemployment reaches
18.7 percent by 2000 and, although declining to 16.4 percent
in 2020, is still at substantially higher levels than those prevailing in 1967. Some decline is noted under lower fertility
rates, but, even under the low assumption, unemployment
declines only very slowly over time, reaching a level of 8.3
percent in 2020. Only under very low fertility is anything

approaching full employment reached, and that only in the
twenty-first century.

The comparison of results obtaining with very high productivity of capital is far more encouraging. Unemployment
declines steadily under all fertility conditions, with faster and
greater progress made as fertility rates are reduced. High
productivity of capital is associated with lower levels of unemployment, but the level of capital productivity in the first
instance is primarily determined by the combination of labor
and capital inputs and of advances in the technological pro-
cesses used in production.

The attempt to reduce unemployment through programs
of fertility reduction is far less circumscribed. A lower rate
of fertility can, to a large extent, offset the effects of a lower
productivity of capital in reducing unemployment. Regardless
of whether the productivity of capital is high or low, lower
rates of fertility are clearly advantageous in providing additional employment, as is shown in Table 35.

Reinforcing the argument for lower fertility is the substantially higher per capita output associated with declines in
fertility. The pattern of gross national product per equivalent
adult consumer using the contribution of employed labor to
output is very similar to estimates based on contributions of
the working age population, as is shown in Table 36. Output
per head under high fertility in 2020 declines to a level of
92.4, compared to 1967 base year values. Medium, low, and
very low fertility assumptions show, by contrast, values of
122.9, 136.9, and 182.0, respectively, as compared to the
base year.

Capital Formation-Relationship
of Demographic and Welfare Investment

Some other indices derived from the economic model
warrant comment. In order to derive net fixed productive
capital formation, it is necessary to net out both demographic
and welfare investment. No demographic investment is made
for the high fertility assumption since no reduction in births
is contemplated. For the other three fertility assumptions,
the numbers of acceptors needed to reduce fertility rates by
1, 2, and 3 percent yearly have been multiplied by an estimated average cost of £J2 ($4.80).

Patterns of costs are most interesting. Even at this
reasonably generous cost estimate level, peak expenditures

TABLE 35

Available and Employed Labor[a] and Estimated Unemployment
Rate, Under Various Fertility Assumptions and Low and High Productivities
of Capital, Jamaica, 1970-2020
(Constant Returns to Scale)

(a)

Low Productivity of Capital (.3)

	High			Medium			Low			Very Low		
Year	Available Labor	Employed Labor	Percent Unemployment	Available Labor	Employed Labor	Percent Unemployment	Available Labor	Employed Labor	Percent Unemployment	Available Labor	Employed Labor	Percent Unemployment
1970	0.782	0.691	11.6	0.782	0.691	11.6	0.782	0.691	11.6	0.782	0.691	11.6
1980	1.127	0.976	13.3	1.127	0.978	13.2	1.127	0.980	13.0	1.127	0.982	12.8
1990	1.621	1.361	16.1	1.614	1.374	14.8	1.605	1.385	13.7	1.596	1.396	12.6
2000	2.417	1.965	18.7	2.310	1.973	14.6	2.214	1.958	11.5	2.113	1.931	8.6
2010	3.574	2.934	17.9	3.185	2.793	12.3	2.816	2.573	8.6	2.443	2.344	4.1
2020	5.268	4.404	16.4	4.197	3.765	10.3	3.396	3.116	8.3	2.437	2.437	0.0

(b)

Very High Productivity of Capital (1.0)

	High			Medium			Low			Very Low		
Year	Available Labor	Employed Labor	Percent Unemployment	Available Labor	Employed Labor	Percent Unemployment	Available Labor	Employed Labor	Percent Unemployment	Available Labor	Employed Labor	Percent Unemployment
1970	0.782	0.703	10.1	0.782	0.703	10.1	0.782	0.703	10.1	0.782	0.703	10.1
1980	1.127	1.023	9.2	1.127	1.024	9.1	1.127	1.026	9.0	1.127	1.027	8.8
1990	1.621	1.470	9.3	1.614	1.475	8.6	1.605	1.478	7.9	1.596	1.481	7.2
2000	2.417	2.193	9.3	2.310	2.144	7.2	2.214	2.090	5.6	2.113	2.028	4.0
2010	3.574	3.277	8.3	3.185	3.009	5.5	2.816	2.719	3.4	2.443	2.415	1.1
2020	5.268	4.866	7.6	4.197	4.022	4.2	3.396	3.302	2.8	2.437	2.437	0.0

[a] In millions.

100

TABLE 36

Gross National Product Per Equivalent Adult Consumer,
No Autonomous Growth, Under Various Fertility
Assumptions, Using Contribution of Employed
Labor to Output, Jamaica, 1970-2020[a]
(Low Productivity of Capital, .3--Constant Returns to Scale)

Year	High	Medium	Low	Very Low
1970	102.6	102.6	102.7	102.7
1980	103.2	104.4	105.6	106.9
1990	98.9	104.7	110.5	117.0
2000	95.0	108.2	121.9	140.0
2010	93.2	114.7	132.3	166.1
2020	92.4	122.9	136.9	182.0

[a]Base 1967=100.

are only slightly more than £2 million. Medium, low, and
very low assumptions have costs almost exactly proportional
to their stated fertility reduction goals until the later part of
this century. After 2000, demographic investment under the
medium reduction program triples, low increases by 50 percent, and very low declines slowly. Two things can be noted:
demographic investment costs are minimal and a substantial
earlier effort in fertility reduction reduces costs later.
Taking the peak expenditure of £2.08 million for the medium
reduction program in 2020, this still represents only .0015
of gross national product. Direct and indirect costs per
acceptor could be more than six times higher before demographic outlays would even hit 1 percent of gross national
product.

The amounts of welfare investment as between fertility
levels reveal some wide differentials. Starting from the same
amount of welfare expenditures in 1970 and incurring higher
outlays for additions to the population, welfare investment
between fertility levels broadens out markedly with time. By
2020, welfare investment under high fertility is 2.7 times as

TABLE 37

Demographic and Welfare Investments, No Autonomous
Growth, Under Various Fertility Assumptions,
Jamaica, 1970-2020
(Low Productivity of Capital--Constant Returns
to Scale--In Millions of Jamaican Pounds)

(a)
Demographic Investment

Year	High	Medium	Low	Very Low
1970	0.00	0.02	0.05	0.07
1980	0.00	0.09	0.18	0.27
1990	0.00	0.30	0.60	0.90
2000	0.00	0.68	1.19	1.89
2010	0.00	1.26	1.49	2.13
2020	0.00	2.08	1.73	1.97

(b)
Welfare Investment

Year	High	Medium	Low	Very Low
1970	13.0	13.0	13.0	13.0
1980	18.5	18.3	18.2	18.0
1990	26.8	25.7	24.6	23.5
2000	39.3	35.3	31.7	27.8
2010	58.0	47.2	39.5	30.3
2020	85.7	60.4	48.0	31.1

great as under very low fertility. There is a cumulative effect of differences for welfare outlays, and these tend to accelerate with time. Both the greatest proportional and absolute increases in such expenditures are registered from 2010 to 2020 under high fertility, as shown in Table 37.

The values generated in the model for welfare investment probably underestimate the differences that would occur in practice. As has been pointed out, the increasing number of relationships involved as organizations or demands grow usually means that the costs of meeting these demands will be more than proportional. The contrasting of productive capital formation under high and very low fertility assumptions indicates that much of the advantage accruing to very low fertility in earlier years is due to lower levels of welfare investment. After the year 2000, however, the increase in gross national product becomes markedly more rapid under very low fertility, with the result that net fixed productive capital formation drops from 7.6 to 5 percent of gross national product and falls to a rate below that of high fertility, as is shown in Table 38.

TABLE 38

Net Fixed Productive Capital Formation as a Proportion
of Gross National Product, Jamaica, 1970-2020
(Constant Returns to Scale--In Percent)

Year	Low Productivity of Capital (.3)	Very High Productivity of Capital (1.0)
1970	7.6	7.6
1980	6.5	7.0
1990	5.9	7.2
2000	5.8	7.6
2010	5.7	7.0
2020	5.7	5.0

TABLE 39

Proportionate Changes in Working-Age Labor Force
and Capital-Labor Ratio, Under Various Fertility
Assumptions, Jamaica, 1970-2020[a]

(a)
Labor Force

Year	High	Medium	Low	Very Low
1970	110.8	110.8	110.8	110.8
1980	157.2	157.2	157.2	157.2
1990	226.4	225.2	224.0	222.9
2000	339.6	324.1	310.3	295.7
2010	502.3	447.1	394.3	341.5
2020	738.0	585.9	473.0	337.3

(b)
Capital-Labor Ratio

Year	High	Medium	Low	Very Low
1970	106.3	106.3	106.3	106.3
1980	117.6	118.1	118.3	118.8
1990	119.2	121.9	124.6	127.2
2000	114.3	123.9	133.7	145.5
2010	111.6	130.8	151.8	182.8
2020	109.8	142.4	171.2	239.5

[a]Base 1967=100.

Capital-Labor Ratio

Product is, of course, also affected by the labor force
and by the relationship of capital to labor (capital-labor ratio).
An increase in labor force, unless accompanied by a proportionate increase in capital, tends to lower the capital-labor
ratio.   For all fertility assumptions, however, capital has
increased faster than labor, and the capital-labor ratio has
become larger.   This effect is particularly marked for the
low and very low fertility projections, because, not only does
the labor force increase more slowly but net additions to
capital stock are at a faster rate.   Differences in fertility assumptions result in no effect on labor force until after 1985
and no substantial effect until after 2000.   This result simply
demonstrates that, for the short run, no program of fertility
reduction will make significant impact on the size of the labor
force, as is shown in Table 39.

CHAPTER **6** CONCLUSIONS

The results of the simulations of the demographic-econometric model provide an insight into the economic consequences of population growth. By revealing clearly the short- and long-run implications of fertility differences, they provide some guidance in determining national policies on population growth, not only for Jamaica but also for other developing countries.

The influence of the growth of population on economic development arises primarily from two effects: changes in the size of the labor force and changes in the age distribution. These effects, in turn, bring about changes in consumption and changes in the rate of net investment.

The model permits comparisons to be made between alternate uses of investment resources. Savings can be used for investment in fixed productive capital stock to produce additional goods and services. Savings can also be used to invest in an effective fertility-reduction program. On the basis of an average cost per contraceptive acceptor and translated into terms of births prevented, a comparison can be made on a per head basis between increases in product (income) and expenditures for fertility reduction.

CHANGE IN SIZE OF LABOR FORCE

The labor force in Jamaica is now increasing much more rapidly than it ever did previously (3 per cent a year). The growth will accelerate through 2000. Reduction in fertility rates will have no substantial influence on the size of labor force until after that time. Up through 1985, this effect is self-evident because entrants into the labor force have already been born, but, even for the additional fifteen years beyond that, the effect is gradual and slow. The great increase in labor force for at least the next thirty years is due to high birth rates in the recent past.

Additions to labor force can also be generated by improvements in mortality. Jamaica is fortunate in this respect, because public health has been improved so that the current expectation of life at birth is sixty-six years. Further, improvements in mortality experience will come more slowly than in the past. The impact of mortality decline, therefore, will make very little difference to the size of the labor force.

By 2020, the projections indicate that some decline in the rate of increase in the size of labor force will occur under medium and low fertility assumption. This notwithstanding, the projected size of labor force fifty years hence is more than sevenfold greater under high fertility and threefold greater under very low fertility than it is at present, as shown in Table 40.

TABLE 40

Labor Force Expressed in Terms of Base
1967= 100, Under Various Fertility Assumptions,
Jamaica, 1970-2020

Year	High	Medium	Low	Very Low
1970	110.8	110.8	110.8	110.8
1980	157.2	157.2	157.2	157.2
1990	226.4	225.2	224.0	222.9
2000	339.6	324.1	310.3	295.7
2010	502.3	447.1	394.3	341.5
2020	737.9	585.9	473.0	337.3

There is present in Jamaica much disguised unemployment and underemployment. Efforts to raise labor input and efficiency, and, thereby, the productivity of the labor force, are met with difficulties of a political, institutional, and attitudinal nature. A rapid increase in the labor force may

aggravate these difficulties in planning for development and
tend to make the social and economic structure more rigid
than it is at present.

In the long run, the absorption of a much larger part of
the labor force into the modern industrial sector may help
raise labor utilization. Some progress in this direction is
indicated by the decline in the percent of labor force in agriculture from 43.8 in 1943 to 37.9 in 1960. Much of the decline, however, represents a movement of labor from rural
areas into urban services and trades. Such movement cannot
be a substitute for absorption into industry since, as in agriculture, the service sector is plagued by underutilization of
labor and low productivity.

Less than 25 percent of the labor force is employed in
the modern industrial sector because much of the industrialization is capital intensive. The most notable example is the
bauxite industry, of which Jamaica is the world's largest
producer. Despite a total investment of £J100 million, only
7,000 workers were employed by it in 1967, including those
in the industry's operations in agriculture. (Under an agree-
ment with the Jamaican government, the bauxite companies
are required to restore the land to agricultural use after the
bauxite has been removed. The companies own one-tenth of
the land in Jamaica and are engaged in large-scale agricultural
operations, particularly cattle-raising.)

In the short run, though, it is not realistic to expect industrialization to take care of the major proportion of the
increase in the labor force. Light industry and import substi-
tution activities predominate--Jamaica lacks coal, iron, and
oil resources. Agriculture will still need to play a dominant
role, particularly if labor utilization can be raised. There is
still considerable opportunity in Jamaica for increasing agricultural output through greater efficiency of work and larger
labor inputs. Land reserves are small, however, and intensi-
fication in the utilization of labor can offer no more than a
breather in the race to keep pace with the increase of the
labor force. Eventually, a situation will be reached where
no further labor can be absorbed by agriculture or only at
very low productivity levels. If industrialization has not by
then reached the level where it can almost totally absorb
the increase in the labor force, stagnation or even retarda-
tion of economic development will be a likely consequence.

CHANGE IN THE AGE STRUCTURE

As was demonstrated in the simulations, high fertility rates impose high dependency burdens. The fifty-year projection for Jamaica under the high assumption gives a dependency ratio around 100 for the entire period. Medium and low fertility assumptions reduce the dependency ratio by well over a third, and, under very low fertility, the dependency ratio is less than thirty.

What this demonstrates is that a reduction in fertility rates has the direct effect of decreasing the dependency burden. There are fewer children to support. The decrease in the proportion of children to adults is progressive as declines in fertility rates are gradually intensified.

The projections also indicate that by 1990, there will be a decline in the relative number of women in the reproductive ages, under medium, low, and very low fertility assumptions. This decline is reversed slightly after 2010, as the age distribution tends to become normalized due to a slight decrease in the percent of people in the productive ages fifteen to sixty-four. The dependency ratio then stabilizes, but at a level far lower than the present high dependency ratio. Given this lower dependency burden, income per head rises.

CHANGE IN CONSUMPTION

It is postulated in the model that consumption increases as gross national product (income) increases after provision for consumption needs of net additions to the population. If the relative shares of private and public consumption are kept at approximately a constant figure, there will be a general rise in the standards of living corresponding to the increase in income per capita.

These are static assumptions and do not take into account the cumulative effects of circular causation. A secondary effect of higher consumption levels may be to increase productivity by increasing both labor input and efficiency. This effect will be of greater importance in the poorest countries, where low levels of nutrition, health, and education affect the efficiency and participation in work. Another factor is that with progressively higher levels of income, the propensity to save can be increased, either through higher levels of voluntary savings or by the government's receiving "forced savings" through taxation. [1] Both forms of saving, when put into direct investment, will tend to increase income per capita, with further cumulative effects as described.

These second-round effects have not been included in the model because they cannot be satisfactorily quantified and the changes that might take place cannot be accurately postulated. In particular, there are some doubts, given the fairly good nutrition and health standards existing in Jamaica, whether improvement in diet would have any appreciable effect on labor productivity. Undoubtedly, with higher levels of income, public expenditures for educational and training facilities can be increased, however, and these could have beneficial effects on productivity in the long run.

The rise in levels of income and consumption indicated in the simulations tend, therefore, to minimize the benefits occurring under reduced fertility assumptions. Despite the conservative bias in suggesting benefits, it is apparent that the effects of reduced rates of population growth are favorable in both economic and human terms and that these effects are very considerable and cumulative, with increased advantage gained over the years.

POPULATION GROWTH RATES AND REQUIRED RATES OF NET INVESTMENT

The significance of rates of population growth can, perhaps, best be demonstrated in relationship to the incremental capital-output ratio, because the product of the two indicates the rate of investment necessary to maintain the current level of per capita output. As a first step, the annual rates of net population growth were computed under all fertility assumptions, as shown in Table 41.

Next, the incremental capital-output ratio (ICOR) was computed for all projections under the four fertility assumptions, four assumptions of capital productivity, and constant returns to scale. Results of the calculations are interesting: (a) ICOR tended to be lower and more stable under high fertility than under conditions of reduced fertility; (b) values of ICOR increased over time under all assumptions, with the greatest increases occurring under lowest fertility assumptions; (c) lower ICOR values were obtained as values of capital productivity increased.

TABLE 41

Annual Net Population Growth Rates
Under Varying Fertility Assumptions,
Jamaica, 1970-2020
(In Percent)

Time Period	High	Medium	Low	Very Low
1970-75	3.48	3.39	3.29	3.20
1975-80	3.69	3.42	3.15	2.86
1980-85	3.72	3.29	2.88	2.41
1985-90	3.76	3.21	2.58	1.89
1990-95	3.79	3.08	2.25	1.27
1995-2000	3.86	3.00	2.12	0.56
2000-2005	3.89	2.77	2.13	0.56
2005-10	3.90	2.57	2.06	0.48
2010-15	3.90	2.35	1.93	0.32
2015-20	3.89	2.11	1.78	0.07

The incremental capital-output ratio is inversely related to the rate of increase of output. For a given increase in output, less additional capital is needed if the ICOR is low than if it is high. This would seem to favor situations of higher population growth, since the value of an additional input of capital relative to the value of an additional input of labor is increasing. This apparent advantage, however, is more than offset by the fact that the higher rates of population growth make less capital available than would prevail under conditions of lower population growth rates.

There is some indication that the current productivity of capital in Jamaica is greater than the low assumption of .3.

When this value is used, annual rates of output are projected between 3 and 4 percent. Between 1953 and 1960, Jamaica had an actual growth rate of 8 percent and a 4.5 percent rate of growth from 1960 to 1966. A medium productivity of capital, .5, gives a much closer approximation to past trends. The ICOR thus obtained averages close to 4.

If the assumption is adopted that the incremental capital-output ratio for Jamaica is four to one (and this is quite probably a low estimate), some indication of the required rates of investment to maintain existing levels of per capita output can be made, as shown in Table 42.

The Jamaican Five-Year Independence Plan, 1963-68, sets a goal of a 5 percent annual rate of growth of gross national product. Actually, the goal is set in terms of gross domestic product at factor cost, but the difference is not significant. If this growth rate were extended for the fifty-year period, about 20 percent of gross national product (growth rate x ICOR) would be needed for net productive investment. Since the proportion of net investment to gross national product averages between 5 and 7 percent over the fifty-year period (see Table 40), it appears that Jamaica will fall far short of reaching the growth goal. Except for very low fertility and the latter stages of low fertility, it seems that net borrowing from abroad will need to be increased just to maintain current per capita income standards. There is, of course, direct connection between the population growth rate of a country and its ability to become self-sufficient in not needing external assistance.

BENEFIT COST ANALYSIS BETWEEN INCREASES IN INCOME PER HEAD AND EXPENDITURES FOR DEMOGRAPHIC INVESTMENT

Some interesting and significant indications of the value of expending resources for fertility reduction as a means of increasing per capita income can be made by means of a simple benefit cost analysis. The basic methodology is to compare, by decades from 1970 to 2020, increases in gross national product on a per head basis under successive fertility assumptions. Differences in the average expenditures per head for demographic investment are determined in the same manner. The ratio of increase in income (gross national product) to increase in demographic investment is then calculated for medium, low, and very low fertility assumptions.

TABLE 42

Required Rates of Net Investment, Under
Varying Fertility Assumptions, Assuming
A Capital-Output Ratio of Four to One,
Jamaica, 1970-2020
(In Percent)

Time Period	High	Medium	Low	Very Low
1970-75	13.92	13.56	13.16	12.80
1975-80	14.76	13.68	12.60	11.44
1980-85	15.00	13.16	11.52	9.64
1985-90	15.04	12.84	10.32	7.56
1990-95	15.16	12.32	10.00	5.08
1995-2000	15.44	12.00	8.48	2.24
2000-2005	15.56	11.08	8.52	2.24
2005-10	15.60	10.28	8.24	1.92
2010-15	15.60	9.40	7.72	1.28
2015-20	15.56	8.44	7.12	0.28

(The high fertility assumption, having no demographic investment, is used only to determine the differences noted under
medium fertility.) This ratio gives a measure of the advantage
to be gained by comparing the increase in national income per
head in relation to the costs needed to bring about each successive level of fertility reduction. Under all assumptions, for
the reduction of fertility, the benefit is cumulative and progressive, well exceeding 200 to 1 by the year 2020. The
greatest advantage lies with medium fertility in the first twenty
years and with low fertility thereafter. At the end of the projection period, however, the ratio under very low fertility is
greater than under medium fertility and increasing at a more
rapid rate than under the other two assumptions.

It should be noted that the analysis is between increases
in income in a given year and expenditures for fertility reduction in the same given year. In consequence, no allowance
for discounting need be made. Increases in income, of course,
are affected by the prevailing capital-labor ratio, which is, in
turn, affected by the amount of fertility reduction previously
incurred. This effect may tend to impart a positive bias,
because the marginal product of capital increases as the relative amount of labor decreases.

Similarly, if costs per acceptor have been underestimated
or increase substantially in the future, the ratio of benefit-
cost would be decreased. The advantage of increases in income relative to increases in expenditures for fertility reduction is still, generally, at least 100 to 1 (i.e., doubling
the cost per acceptor reduces the advantage in half). Under
any circumstances, however, the payoff is so tremendous in
favor of expending resources for fertility reduction that the
justification for such policy is unaffected, as shown in Table
43.

ENVIRONMENTAL CONSTRAINTS

The results of the simulations in this study suggest the
magnitude of the consequences of population growth in other
more general areas relating to economic development. The
failure to solve these concomitant problems will directly
affect the likelihood of Jamaica's remaining a viable political
entity, capable of providing a better life for its citizens.

The fifty-year projection under high fertility gives an
estimated population of Jamaica of 14 million in 2020. This

TABLE 43

Change in Gross National Product Per Equivalent Consumer
Relative to Change in Demographic Investment Per Equivalent
Consumer, as Between Levels of Fertility Reduction, Jamaica,
1980-2020

Year	Medium Fertility			Low Fertility			Very Low Fertility		
	Change in GNP (ΔY)	Change in Demographic Investment (ΔDI)	Relative Change ($\Delta Y/\Delta DI$)	Change in GNP (ΔY)	Change in Demographic Investment (ΔDI)	Relative Change ($\Delta Y/\Delta DI$)	Change in GNP (ΔY)	Change in Demographic Investment (ΔDI)	Relative Change ($\Delta Y/\Delta DI$)
1980	2.1	0.019	110.5	2.1	0.021	110.0	2.2	0.021	104.8
1990	9.6	0.062	154.8	9.9	0.065	152.3	11.1	0.078	142.3
2000	19.1	0.106	180.2	21.4	0.118	181.4	29.2	0.198	147.5
2010	31.8	0.153	207.8	26.1	0.091	286.8	52.9	0.272	194.5
2020	46.2	0.207	223.2	19.2	0.060	319.4	60.0	0.253	236.8

means that for every person living in Jamaica today, there
will be seven persons fifty years hence. Density on this comparatively small island would increase from 475 to 3,325
persons per square mile.[2] Such population density would be
five times that currently existing in Japan and would imply
an almost totally urbanized island.

At present, tourism is the third most important source
of economic livelihood in Jamaica and is extremely important
as a source of foreign exchange. If, however, population
were to increase anywhere near the high or even medium
projections, it is doubtful whether the tourist industry could
continue in anything like its present form. The attraction of
Jamaica lies, primarily, in the clear waters and clean
beaches of its shores. It is doubtful that the comparatively
pollution-free setting can be maintained in the face of greatly
increased population pressures.

There will almost certainly have to be tighter social controls on many activities. Traffic may become so dense that
the use of private automobiles may have to be curtailed.
Already, Kingston has adopted complex traffic controls, and
this is only the beginning of what may be ahead.

Pollution

Controls over water and air pollution, now virtually non-
existent, will also have to become strict. Jamaica, already
suffering from water shortages, will have to increase greatly
the efficiency with which water is used and reused. Industrial
plants that pollute water substantially will have to be zoned
into areas so that they become the last in line to use it. As
population grows, air pollution will intensify. Much of this
pollution originates near major urban areas, as witness the
production in cement, gypsum, and refined petroleum
products, all within the immediate Kingston area. A disper-
sion of industrial plants away from major cities in the future
may help, but, when overall population density rises, such
unencumbered areas become harder to find. Even now,
Spanishtown, the original capital of Jamaica, is finding that
much of its air has been polluted from emissions coming
from Kingston. This is likely to be aggravated in the future
because of the east-west chain of mountains that separates the
coastal areas of Jamaica. The pollution that is carried in-
land in the mornings is likely to be returned with the prevailing
seaward winds of the evening.

Energy Demands

Another major problem that Jamaica will be facing in
the future is the increased demand for energy.   The present
rate of population growth in Jamaica implies a doubling
approximately every twenty-one years, but consumption of
energy has been doubling every seven years--10 percent
annual rate of increase.[3] Future demands will be increased,
not only by population growth but also by economic development.

Jamaica does not possess any known commercial quantities of fossil fuel resources. Energy is generated by hydro-
electric power and by steam plants fueled by imported petroleum. Additional hydro sources are limited, and, even now,
water shortages during the dry season have caused brownouts
and cuts in electric service. The prospect would be for increasing importation of fossil fuels, with consequent unfavor-
able impact on the balance of payments.

Worldwide, the era of fossil fuel consumption will be
drawing to a close in a relatively short time. The United
States, which is extremely favored in its reserves of fossil
fuels, has been estimated to have resources for no longer
than sixty years.[4] Estimates of world reserves are subject
to somewhat greater error, since knowledge of what or where
such reserves actually exist is not full. The rate of growth
of demand for fossil fuels is also uncertain. It would be safe
to surmise that, in practically all countries, projected demand for power is likely to be underestimated. (The wide-
spread underestimates of projected energy use in the United
States by utility companies reinforce this belief.)

Technological developments may, in time, make direct
tapping of solar energy practicable as a source of power.
Most likely, however, nuclear power plants will become the
major energy source for Jamaica. While operating costs of
plants using atomic energy are now relatively low, the initial
costs of building such plants are quite high, because added
to construction costs are the interest payments on the enor-
mous uranium inventory needed for production of atomic energy.
It has been estimated that if interest on capital is five percent
yearly, the annual cost on uranium inventories is twenty-five
times the cost of the uranium consumed.[5] The purchase of
the requisite uranium inventory highlights the general importance of finding the means to increase capital investment.
The transition to nuclear power will require large amounts of
capital and will be made much more difficult if rates of population growth continue to be high.

Production of atomic energy also requires far more
careful and costly measures to control its wastes. The dis-
posal of such wastes has not always been carried out efficiently
in the past, and concern is increasing, particularly for plants
located near populated areas. The effects of radiation leakage
are far more pervasive and lethal than pollution caused by
fossil fuel burning. Also, the effect of thermal pollution,
caused by the heating of the water used in the production of
energy, is considerably greater than for existing steam plants.
The raising of the temperature of lakes and streams promotes
the growth of algae at the expense of oxygen-producing diatoms,
thus having consequences in overall oxygen supply.

Food

Much of the present agricultural production in Jamaica
is in export crops, notably sugar and bananas. An increase
in population raises the question of how export agriculture
can be continued when demands for foodstuffs for domestic
markets increase. Except for greater exploitation of the seas
surrounding it, Jamaica, like all countries, can increase
food production through expansion of agricultural acreage or
by means of a greater yield per acre.

As of 1960, approximately 88 per cent of potential cropland in Jamaica was being utilized for agricultural production. [6]
In the past, some increase in cropland has occurred at the expense of forest and pasture land and has caused certain un-
desirable side effects by increasing erosion and water runoff.
Irrigation is being used in the cultivation of sugarcane, but
has not come into general use for domestically consumed
agricultural products. There are some semiarid regions in
Jamaica that could be put into production, assuming the capital for irrigation systems can be found. Approximately 80
percent of the country is mountainous and, except for a small
amount of subsistence farming, is not suitable for agricultural
production.

A higher rate of population growth necessitates greater
food production, while, at the same time, continuously reducing
cropland by urbanization. (This effect is particularly notable
in Jamaica in the closing of sugar estates in the vicinity of
Kingston.) If export agriculture can be increased and at
profitable prices, some of the demand for local foodstuffs
can be met by using the balances for increased food imports.
There are some risks in such a strategy, however. The fact

that developing countries like Jamaica are exporters of raw
materials or primary agriculture products means that the
prices of what they export are largely dictated by world conditions, while what they import is somewhat more subject to
administered prices. Given this situation, evidence seems
to support the theory that the terms of trade are increasingly
disadvantageous to the developing countries.

This notwithstanding, if export agriculture is displaced
by using those croplands for domestic production, there is
still a large gap in needed foreign exchange. Presently, the
large-scale organization implicit in the agricultural export
sector is fairly efficiently organized. The conversion to
domestic crop production is unlikely to produce the economies
of scale now present. Pressures of population growth are
likely to increase demands for ownership of land by individual
farmers. The breaking up of large-scale estates (Bolivia is
a notable example) has resulted in a decline of both aggregate
and per acre yields.

The second means cited for increasing food production is
increasing the yield per acre of land already in cultivation.
Certainly fertilizer, insecticides, and improved strains will
increase crop yields. All these methods, however, require
increased financial outlays. Farmers will need to be taught
the benefits of using improved methods and agricultural extension workers will be required. Provisions will also be
needed for increasing availability of credit and better means
of storage and distribution, particularly in the more remote
areas.

Increasing food production necessitates more ample supplies of water. Jamaica, possessing a warm climate, could
engage in double-cropping, providing that a year-round
system of water is supplied. Increased consumption of water,
because of population growth as well as by industrial development, will tend to cut into available supplies of water for
agriculture. If groundwater is resorted to on an increasing
scale, groundwater levels will tend to decline steadily, because such a resource is not automatically replenished. A
possible solution to the water supply problem is desalinization
of sea water. The cost of this process elsewhere is now so
great that desalinization is used only for drinking water and
not for agriculture. Even with a sharp reduction in cost,
agricultural use would probably be restricted to coastal areas,
since the cost of transport over longer distances and higher
elevations would be unduly expensive.

A final consideration is that yields of food per acre can

also be improved considerably if reduced use is made of protein from animal sources. From five to eight calories of plant food are needed to produce one calorie of foodstuff obtained by human beings from animals.[7] Food from animal sources is extremely wasteful of plant calories, and this is the reason why in the very poorest countries, little food comes from such sources. To eat lower on the food chain is not necessarily the most desirable alternative (particularly, if numbers of people have inadequate diet due to insufficient protein), but elimination of animal-source foodstuffs can be an interim measure. The need to do is, of course, directly related to the pressures of population growth.

It has been estimated that in order to raise the nutritional standards of the world to acceptable levels, additional supplies would have to be about 3.5 times as large as current world food production. The level of nutrition in Jamaica is probably much better than that in most developing countries, but there are no hard data on what proportion or how many persons in Jamaica are now malnourished. Adequacy of diet is enhanced by Jamaica's favorable location in relation to the sea and resultant availability of protein from fish. However, some increase in food production to raise existing levels of nutrition is, nonetheless, indicated.

The possibilities of increasing food production in the long run are very great. The critical variable, however, is time. Such an expansion would require massive amounts of capital, materials, and energy, all of which are in short supply. Further, scientific and technological progress is needed, and this, too, requires time. Failing this, costs of food production can be expected to rise in the near future.

The environmental constraints of pollution, water, energy, and food can be ameliorated by reducing the pressures caused by population growth. Measures to control pollution, ensure adequate water supplies, produce energy, or increase food output all require higher levels of technology and greater capital investments. To the extent that faster growth of population increases consumption at the expense of resources that could be used for these investments, the problems are intensified. The need to provide for additional people creates the problems, while, at the same time, reducing the resources that could be made available for solving the problems.

OTHER APPLICATIONS

Many applications can be made from this model for
planning purposes. One of the most useful is in preparing
estimates of expenditures for welfare outlays, particularly
in education, health, and public housing.

Demands for education services can be assessed in
terms of the numbers of teachers and classrooms required
to meet changes in population growth. Health services are
needed by all sectors of the population and require additional
medical personnel and hospital clinics. Public housing is
affected by replacements to existing public housing, demands
for construction due to current housing deficits, and demands
generated by additions to the current population.

Most developing countries are dependent to a considerable
extent on external capital assistance in order to promote
economic development. A useful extension of the model,
therefore, is to input desired growth goals (i.e., 5 percent
annual increase in gross national product or 3 percent increase in gross national product per capita) and to determine
how much investment will be needed to produce these goals.
To reduce and, eventually, eliminate dependency on external
capital assistance will require reduction in fertility rates.
Just how much and how rapidly these reductions should be in
order to achieve stipulated growth levels can be determined
from the model.

RECOMMENDATIONS

Population policy should be regarded as an integral part
of economic policy. There is a great need for strong and
coordinated efforts in population planning and all other planning
if the challenge of the future is to be met. In developing
countries particularly, the two special reasons for the urgency
in undertaking and effectively implementing a policy of reducing population growth without delay are that reductions in
fertility rates can be brought about only gradually and that the
exceptionally large proportion of young dependents under
prevailing fertility rates offsets much of the potential reduction in births which results from lowered fertility rates.

The economic advantages to be derived from devoting
sufficient resources to reduce fertility rates as rapidly as

possible are compelling. Since these advantages are cumulative and progressive, the ultimate benefits are greater, the
sooner fertility reduction occurs. The alternatives of doing
nothing or making only limited efforts is to deprive a country
of the opportunity to increase substantially the living standards
of its peoples. When coupled with environmental constraints,
failure to act forcefully to reduce population growth threatens
not only the economic and social viability of a country but
even its continued existence as a political entity.

NOTES

1. Harvey Leibenstein, Economic Backwardness and
Economic Growth (New York: John Wiley and Sons, Inc.,
1957), pp. 62-69.

2. Donald J. Bogue, Principles of Demography (New
York: John Wiley and Sons, Inc., 1969), p. 64.

3. Jamaica Ministry of Development and Welfare Five
Year Independence Plan 1963-1968 (Kingston, 1963), p. 66.

4. Harrison Brown, The Challenge of Man's Future
(New York: Viking Press, 1954), p. 164.

5. Ibid., p. 176.

6. Five Year Independence Plan 1963-1968, p. 18.

7. Georg Borgstrom, The Hungry Planet (New York:
Macmillan, 1965), p. 28.

BIBLIOGRAPHY

BIBLIOGRAPHY

Abbott, George C. "Estimates of the Growth of the Population of the West Indies to 1975," Social and Economic
Studies, 12 (September, 1963), pp. 236-45.

Belshaw, Horace. Population Growth and Levels of Consumption. London: George Allen and Unwin, 1956.

Bethel, Jeannette. "Some National Income Aggregates for
Jamaica at Constant Prices," Social and Economic
Studies, 10 (June, 1961), pp. 128-55.

Blake, Judith. "Family Instability and Reproductive Behavior
in Jamaica: Current Research in Human Fertility,"
The Milbank Memorial Fund Quarterly, XXXIII (January,
1955), 24-41.

Bogue, Donald J. Principles of Demography. New York:
John Wiley and Sons, Inc., 1969.

Borgstrom, Georg. The Hungry Planet. New York: Macmillan, 1965.

Bourgeois-Pichat, Jean. Population Growth and Development.
New York: Carnegie Endowment for International Peace,
1966.

Bower, Leonard G. "The Return from Investment in Population Control in Less-Developed Countries," Demography,
V, 1 (1968), 422-32.

Brown, Harrison. The Challenge of Man's Future. New York:
Viking Press, 1954.

Chen, Kuan-I. World Population Growth and Living Standards.
New York: Bookman Associates, 1960.

Chenery, Hollis B., and Alan M. Strout. "Foreign Assistance
    and Economic Development," The American Economic
    Review, LVI, 4 (September, 1966), 679-733.

Clark, Colin. Population Growth and Land Use. New York:
    Macmillan-St. Martin's Press, Inc., 1967.

Coale, Ansley J. "Population and Economic Development,"
    The Population Dilemma. Edited by Philip M. Hauser.
    Princeton, N.J.: Princeton University Press, 1958.

_____, and Paul Demeny. Regional Model Life Tables.
    Princeton, N.J.: Princeton University Press, 1966.

_____, and Edgar M. Hoover. Population Growth and
    Economic Development in Low Income Countries.
    Princeton, N.J.: Princeton University Press, 1958.

Cumper, George E. Preliminary Analysis of Population
    Growth and Social Characteristics in Jamaica, 1943-1960.
    Kingston: Institute of Social and Economic Research,
    University of the West Indies, 1964.

Currie, Lauchlin. Obstacles to Development. East Lansing,
    Mich.: Michigan State University Press, 1967.

Davis, Kingsley. "Population Policy: Will Current Programs
    Succeed?," Science, 158 (Nov. 10, 1967), pp. 730-39.

Demas, William G. The Economics of Development in Small
    Countries With Special Reference to the Caribbean.
    Montreal: McGill University Press, 1965.

Demeny, Paul. "The Economics of Population Control."
    Paper presented at Annual Meeting of the International
    Union for the Scientific Study of Population, London,
    September 3-10, 1969.

_____. "Investment Allocation and Population Growth,"
    Demography, II (1965), 203-32.

Easterlin, Richard A. "Effects of Population Growth on the
    Economic Development of Developing Countries," The
    Annals of the American Academy of Political and Social
    Science, 369 (January, 1967), pp. 98-108.

Enke, Stephen. "Birth Control for Economic Development,"
Science, 164 (May 16, 1969), pp. 798-802.

_____. "The Economic Aspects of Slowing Population
Growth," The Economic Journal, LXXVI (March, 1966),
44-56.

_____. Economics for Development. Englewood
Cliffs, N.J.: Prentice-Hall, 1963.

_____. Lower Birth Rates--Some Economic Aspects.
Washington, D.C.: United States Agency for International
Development, 1965.

_____, et al. Economic Benefits of Slowing Population
Growth. (68TMP-122). Santa Barbara, Calif.: TEMPO,
General Electric Center for Advanced Studies, 1969.

_____. Manual for Calculation of Government Expendi-
tures for Selected Social Services. (68TMP-121). Santa
Barbara, Calif.: TEMPO, General Electric Center for
Advanced Studies, 1969.

_____. Population Growth and Economic Development:
Background and Guide. (68TMP-119). Santa Barbara,
Calif.: TEMPO, General Electric Center for Advanced
Studies, 1969.

Enke, Stephen (General Editor), and William E. McFarland,
et al. Description of the Economic Demographic Model.
(68TMP-120). Santa Barbara, Calif.: TEMPO, General
Electric Center for Advanced Studies, 1969.

Enke, Stephen, and Richard G. Zind. "Effect of Fewer
Births on Average Income," Journal of Biosocial Sci-
ences, I, 1 (1969), 41-55. Originally published by Enke
as Raising Per Capita Income Through Fewer Births.
Santa Barbara, Calif.: TEMPO, General Electric
Center for Advanced Studies, 1967.

Ericksen, E. Gordon. The West Indies Population Problem.
Social Science Studies. Lawrence, Kans.: University of
Kansas Publications, 1962.

Fox, Gerald L. "The Net Costs to Society of a Marginal
    Birth in Underdeveloped Countries." Paper presented
    at Annual Meeting of the Population Association of
    America, Atlantic City, N.J., April 12, 1969.

Harewood, Jack. "Overpopulation and Underemployment in
    the West Indies," International Labour Review, LXXXII,
    2 (August, 1960), 103-37.

_____. "Recent Population Trends and Family Planning
    Activity in the Caribbean Area," Demography, V, 2
    (1968), 874-93.

Heer, David M. "Economic Development and Fertility,"
    Demography, III, 2 (1966), 423-44.

Hoover, Edgar M. "Economic Consequences of Population
    Growth." Pittsburgh: University of Pittsburgh, 1965.
    (Mimeographed.)

_____, and Mark Perlman. "Measuring the Effects of
    Population Control on Economic Development: Pakistan
    as a Case Study," Pakistan Development Review, VI, 4
    (Winter, 1966), pp. 545-66.

Horlacher, David E. "Measuring the Economic Benefits of
    Population Control: A Critical Review of the Literature."
    Penn State-USAID Working Paper No. 2. Washington,
    D.C.: United States Agency for International Develop-
    ment, 1968.

International Bank for Reconstruction and Development. The
    Economic Development of Jamaica. Baltimore: The
    Johns Hopkins Press, 1952.

Jaffe, A. J. People, Jobs and Economic Development.
    Glencoe, Ill.: The Free Press, 1959.

Jamaica Central Planning Unit. Economic Survey Jamaica,
    1959; 1960; 1961; 1963; 1965; 1966; 1967. Kingston: The
    Government Printer, 1960, 1961, 1962, 1964, 1966,
    1967, 1968.

Jamaica Department of Statistics. Annual Abstract of
    Statistics, 1954-68. Kingston, 1954-68.

_____ . Employment and Earnings in Large Establishments, 1965. Kingston, 1967.

_____ . Industrial Activity, Mining, Manufacture, Construction, 1960. Kingston, 1963.

_____ . National Accounts: Income and Expenditure,
1950-1957, 1958, 1959, 1960, 1961. Kingston, 1958-62.

_____ . National Income and Product, 1959-1962; 1964;
1965-1966; 1967. Kingston, 1963, 1965, 1967, 1968.

_____ . (O. C. Francis). The People of Jamaica.
Kingston, 1963.

_____ . Quarterly Abstract of Statistics, Nos. 1-36.
Kingston, 1961-69.

Jamaica Ministry of Development and Welfare. Five Year
Independence Plan 1963-1968. Kingston, 1963.

Jamaica Registrar General. Demographic Statistics Of
Jamaica, 1964, 1967. Spanishtown, 1965, 1968.

Jones, Gavin W. The Economic Effect of Declining Fertility
in Less Developed Countries. New York: Population
Council, 1969.

_____ , and Gingrich, Paul. "The Effects of Differing
Trends in Fertility and of Educational Advance on the
Growth, Quality, and Turnover of the Labor Force,"
Demography, V, 1 (1968), 226-48.

Keyfitz, Nathan. World Population. Chicago: University of
Chicago Press, 1968.

Kleiman, E. "Age Composition, Size of Households, and the
Interpretation of Per Capita Income," Economic Development and Cultural Change, XV, 1 (October, 1966), 37-58.

Kuznets, Simon. "Demographic Aspects of Modern Economic
Growth." Working paper of the World Population Conference in Belgrade, 1965. WPC/WP/389.

_____ . Economic Growth and Structure; Selected
Essays. New York: W. W. Norton & Co., 1965.

_____. "Population and Economic Growth, " Proceedings of the American Philosophical Society, III, 3 (June, 1967), 170-93.

Leibenstein, Harvey. Economic Backwardness and Economic Growth. New York: John Wiley and Sons, Inc., 1957.

_____. "Pitfalls in Benefit-Cost Analysis of Birth Prevention, " Population Studies, XXIII, 2 (July, 1969), 161-70.

Lloyd, Peter. "A Growth Model with Population and Technological Change as Endogenous Variables." Unpublished paper, 1968, excerpted by Warren C. Robinson and David E. Horlacher in "Evaluating the Economic Benefits of Fertility Reduction," Studies in Family Planning, 39 (March, 1969), pp. 4-8.

Meier, Richard L. Modern Science and the Human Fertility Problem. New York: John Wiley and Sons, Inc., 1959.

Myrdal, Gunnar. Asian Drama. 3 vols. New York: Pantheon Books Division of Random House, 1968.

Newman, Peter, and R. H. Allen. Population Growth Rates and Economic Development in Nicaragua. Washington, D.C.: Robert R. Nathan Associates, Inc., 1967.

Ohlin, Goran. Population Control and Economic Development. Paris: Development Center of the Organization for Economic Cooperation and Development, 1967.

O'Loughlin, Carleen. "Long Term Growth of the Economy of Jamaica," Social and Economic Studies, XII, 3 (September, 1963), 246-82.

Roberts, George W. The Population of Jamaica. Cambridge: Cambridge University Press, 1957.

Robinson, Warren C. "Conceptual and Methodological Problems Connected with Cost-Effectiveness Studies of Family Planning Programs" Penn-State-USAID Working Paper No. 1. Washington, D.C.: United States Agency for International Development, 1968.

_____, et al. "A Cost-Effectiveness Analysis of Selected
Family Planning Programs." (Under Penn State-USAID
Population Project). University Park, Pa.: Pennsylvania
State Department of Economics, 1969.

Robinson, Warren C. and David E. Horlacher. "Evaluating
the Economic Benefits of Fertility Reduction," Studies
in Family Planning, 39 (March, 1969), pp. 4-8.

Ruprecht, Theodore K. "Fertility Control, Investment and
Per Capita Output: A Demographic Econometric Model
of the Philippines." Contributed Papers. International
Union for the Scientific Study of Population, Sydney Conference, August 21-25, 1967. Pp. 98-107.

Segal, Aaron. Politics and Population in the Caribbean. Rio
Piedras, Puerto Rico: Institute of Caribbean Studies,
University of Puerto Rico, 1969.

Senior, Clarence. "Demography and Economic Development,"
Social and Economic Studies, VII, 3 (September, 1958),
9-23.

Simon, J. L. "The Value of Avoided Births to Underdeveloped
Countries." Unpublished paper, 1967, summarized by
David E. Horlacher in "Measuring the Economic Benefits
of Population Control: A Critical Review of the Literature." Penn State-USAID Working Paper No. 2. Washington, D. C.: United States Agency for International
Development, 1968. Pp. 43-45.

Sovani, N. W. "Relations Between Population Pressure and
Economic and Demographic Change." Paper presented
at meeting of the International Union for the Scientific
Study of Population, London, September 3-10, 1969.

Spengler, Joseph J. "The Economics of Population Growth."
The Population Crisis and the Use of World Resources.
Edited by Stuart Mudd. Bloomington, Ind.: Indiana
University Press, 1964.

_____. "The Economist and the Population Question,"
The American Economic Review, LVI, 1 (March, 1966),
1-24.

Stockwell, Edward G. "Some Demographic Correlates of
    Economic Development," Rural Sociology, 31 (June,
    1966), pp. 216-24.

Stone, Richard. "Input-Output and Demographic Accounting:
    A Tool for Educational Planning," Minerva, IV (Spring,
    1966), 365-80.

Tachi, Ninoru, and Yoichi Okazaki. "Economic Development
    and Population Growth--With Special Reference to South-
    east Asia," The Developing Economies, 3 (December,
    1965), pp. 497-515.

Tekse, Kalman. A Note on the Increasing Fertility of
    Jamaica's Population. Kingston: Department of Statis-
    tics, 1967.

_____. A Study of Fertility in Jamaica. Kingston:
    Department of Statistics, 1968.

Thorne, Alfred P. Size, Structure and Growth of the Economy
    of Jamaica. Kingston: Institute of Social and Economic
    Research, University of the West Indies, 1955.

United Nations, Department of Economic and Social Affairs.
    Age and Sex Patterns of Mortality: Model Life-Tables
    for Under-Developed Countries. Population Studies, No.
    22. (ST/SOA/Ser.A). New York: 1955.

_____. Demographic Aspects of Manpower, Report I:
    Sex and Age Patterns of Participation in Economic Activi-
    ties. Population Studies No. 33. (ST/SOA/Ser.A).
    New York: 1962.

_____. Demographic Yearbook, 1948-1967. New York:
    1949-68.

_____. The Future Growth of World Population. Popu-
    lation Studies No. 28. (ST/SOA/Ser. A). New York: 1958.

_____. General Principles for National Programmes of
    Population Projections as Aids to Development Planning.
    Population Studies No. 38. (ST/SOA/Ser.A). New York:
    1965.

_____ . Methods of Appraisal of Quality of Basic Data for Population Estimates. Manual II, Population Studies No. 23. (ST/SOA/Ser.A). New York: 1955.

_____ . Methods of Estimating Basic Demographic Measures from Incomplete Data. Manual IV, Population Studies No. 42. (ST/SOA/Ser.A). New York: 1967.

_____ . Methods for Population Projections by Sex and Age. Manual III, Population Studies No. 25. (ST/SOA/Ser.A). New York: 1956.

_____ . National Programmes of Analysis of Population Census Data as an Aid to Planning and Policy-Making. Population Studies No. 36. (ST/SOA/Ser.A). New York: 1964.

_____ . Population Growth and the Standard of Living in Under-Developed Countries. Population Studies No. 20. (ST/SOA/Ser.A). New York: 1954.

_____ . World Population Prospects as Assessed in 1963. Population Studies No. 41. (ST/SOA/Ser.A). New York: 1966.

United Nations, Department of Social Affairs. The Determinants and Consequences of Population Trends. Population Studies No. 17. (ST/SOA/Ser.A). New York: 1953.

United Nations, Economic Commission for Latin America. Human Resources of Central America, Panama and Mexico, 1950-1980, in Relation to Some Aspects of Economic Development. (ST/TAO/k/LAT.1). New York: 1960.

United Nations, Economic and Social Council. "Inquiry Among Governments on Problems Resulting from the Interaction of Economic Development and Population Changes." Report of the Secretary-General. (E/3895/Rev.1). New York: 1964.

United Nations World Population Conference. Proceedings, 1965. 4 vols. New York: 1967. (E/CONF. 4113, Sales No.: 66 XIII. 6.)

United States Agency for International Development. Effects of Population Growth on Economic and Social Development in Thailand. Bangkok: United States Operations Mission, 1967.

University of the West Indies. "Estimates of Intercensal Population by Age and Sex and Revised Vital Rates for British Caribbean Countries, 1946-1960." Census Research Program Publication No. 8. Kingston, 1964.

_____. "Life Tables for British Caribbean Countries, 1959-1961." Census Research Program Publication No. 9. Kingston, 1965.

Van de Walle, E. "An Operation Index of Overpopulation," Economic Development and Cultural Change, 14 (October, 1965), pp. 91-93.

Zaidan, George. "The Foregone Benefits and Costs of a Prevented Birth: Conceptual Problems and an Application to the U.A.R." Economics Department Working Paper No. 11. Washington, D.C.: International Bank for Reconstruction and Development, 1968.

_____. "Population Growth and Economic Development," Studies in Family Planning, No. 42 (May, 1969), pp. 1-6. Revision of article first appearing in Finance and Development (March, 1969), pp. 2-8.

_____, and E. K. Hawkins. "The Treatment of Population in Bank Economic Work." Economics Department Working Paper No. 16. Washington, D.C.: International Bank for Reconstruction and Development, 1968.

ABOUT THE AUTHOR

B. Thomas Walsh is Associate Professor of Demography at the Graduate School of Public Health, University of Pittsburgh. As an economist and a demographer, he is particularly concerned with the economic implications of population growth in its international dimensions.

Dr. Walsh worked for a number of years with the United States Agency for International Development. Following his first overseas assignment in the Philippines as an adviser in civil service and community development, he served as Chief of the Public Administration Division in Bolivia, the Dominican Republic, and Panama. At the latter two posts, he also doubled as Population Officer, devoting much of his time in helping to establish voluntary and public programs in family planning.

Dr. Walsh studied economics and public administration at Syracuse University. His postgraduate work was done at the Maxwell School of Citizenship and Public Affairs at Syracuse and at the University of Pittsburgh, where he completed his doctoral program.